Hidden Wealth in SME stocks: Guide to SME Stocks of the Indian Market

A BOOK WRITTEN BY

CA ANSHUL KARWA

Source ISBN : 978-1-9994163-7-9

Version: 2024-03-07

Table of contents

Thank You Note _____ 1

Story Behind Writing this Book_____ 2

About the Author_____ 4

Chapter1: Brief overview of the significance of SMEs in India's economy 7

Explanation of the purpose and potential benefits of investing in SME stocks_____ 12

Types of Companies Based on Size Market Cap Categories: Small, Mid, and Large: _____ 16

Chapter 2: Introduction to the stock market and how it functions_____ 19

Key terms and concepts: stocks, IPOs, market capitalization _____ 24

How stock prices are determined? _____ 31

Discussion on the potential risks and rewards associated with SME stocks _____ 37

Factors influencing stock prices in the SME segment _____ 46

Chapter 3: Real life case studies of successful SME stocks _____ 56

Chapter 4: IPOs and the SME Segment_ 77

Understanding Initial Public Offerings (IPOs) and their significance _____ 78

The IPO process for SMEs in India_____ 81

Chapter 5: How to Evaluate SME Stocks 87

Fundamental analysis for SME stocks_____ 88

Chapter 6: Building a Portfolio with SME Stocks _____ 107

Diversification strategies for incorporating SME stocks in a portfolio_____ 108

Balancing risk and return with SME investments _____ 112

Chapter 7: Case studies of well-structured SME stock portfolios _____ 117

Chapter 8: Government Initiatives and Regulations _____ 125

Overview of government schemes supporting SMEs and their impact on stocks _____ 126

Impact of Government Initiatives on Stocks: ___ 134

Regulatory considerations for investors in SME stocks _____ 139

Chapter 9: Tips for Successful SME Stock Investing_____ 145

Practical tips and advice for individuals looking to invest in SME stocks _____ 146

Avoid these common traps _____ 150

Real life examples:_____ 153

Chapter 10: Learning from experienced investors in the SME segment_____ 158

Chapter 11: How I Select and Invest in SME Stocks _____ 175

Chapter 12: My Top 10 Picks of SME Stocks _____ 180

Conclusion _____ 189

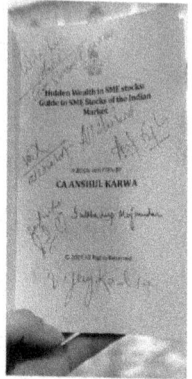

Thank You Note

This book is dedicated to all the hardworking entrepreneurs, investors, and traders who dare to think differently and explore the world of SME stocks.

To every business owner whether small or big who has built something from the ground level, your hard work and ideas inspire many others.

To the investors who take the road less travelled, to find the hidden gems in the market, you are the reason SMEs grow.

A special thank you to my parents, mentors, and friends who have always believed in me. Your help, motivation, and advice have guided me, and I will always be thankful for that.

This book is for you, with respect, gratitude, and a shared dream of finding hidden wealth.

Story Behind Writing this Book

The story behind this book begins with a simple realization back in 2021: I didn't know much about SMEs (Small and Medium Enterprises). As I stepped into the world of SME's, I was amazed to learn how these small companies were securing funds and steadily growing. What surprised me even more was the impressive returns few investors were making compared to mid and large cap stocks.

After studying SMEs in depth and analysing a few stocks, I took the risk and invested. To my surprise, my first investment gave me an amazing 185% return in just 5-6 months (we will further see in this book about that stock and other stocks). This success motivated me to learn more about the SME market.

For the next two years, I had put myself in research and testing, aiming to find the hidden potential of this SME market.

Through this book, I want to make people aware that the SME market is for everyone and it is not as risky as people think. My goal is to show the great opportunities in SMEs and encourage people to explore and invest in this growing market.

We'll begin by covering the fundamentals, from understanding what SMEs are, to the criteria for selecting the right ones. Moving forward, we'll study into real life case studies, providing practical insights and case studies on how to identify and choose promising SMEs for investment and to get insights of my personal portfolio.

About the Author

Hi, I am Anshul Karwa, a Practicing Chartered Accountant by profession and passionate about simplifying the complexities and find the hidden treasures of the stock market. With additional qualifications in Law, and Computer Applications, I bring a strong expertise in finance, law, and technology to my work.

Experience: I have over nine years of experience in stock market investing, I have seen both bear and bull phases. This experience has given me a strong understanding of how the market works, helping me handle challenges and make the most of opportunities.

Corporate Experience: I have worked with renowned multinational corporations such as Deloitte and JSW, where I learned and used my financial insights in diverse and challenging environments.

My Mission: My goal is to guide and help people with smart financial decisions through my book "Hidden Wealth in SME stocks: Guide to SME Stocks of the Indian Market". My goal is to offer practical lessons through case studies and my positions, drawn from real stock market experiences, to guide readers towards informed and successful investing.

Get in early with a growing company and ride the wave of success together.
-

CA ANSHUL KARWA

Chapter1: Brief overview of the significance of SMEs in India's economy

The Economic Impact of SMEs in India

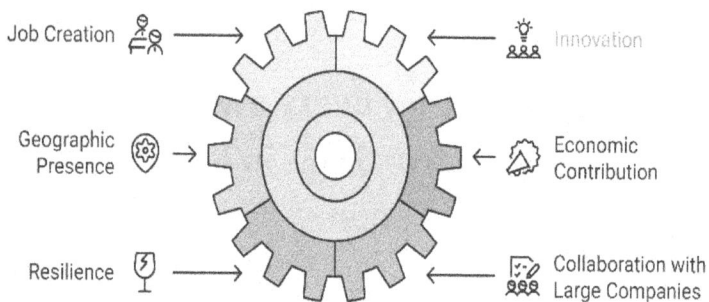

Hidden Wealth in SME Stocks
By
CA ANSHUL KARWA

8

We can say that SMEs are like the unsung heroes of the Indian economy. They are businesses that are not big companies but they are still super important. Let me break down why it matters:

1. Job Creator: SMEs are machines which provide jobs to many people, from cities to quiet villages. So, if you hear about someone starting a new business, chances are it is a SME or maybe below.

2. Creative Thinkers: These businesses are like think tanks. They always think of cool new things. Sometimes the next big thing starts as a small business idea. SMEs are like innovators in the business world.

3. Everywhere, for everyone: SMEs are not picky about where to set up shop.

You can find them all over the country. This leads to growth and positive development in many areas, not just cities.

4. Money drivers: When you add up all the small contributions from SMEs, it's like throwing a big party for the economy. Together they generate capital, which is a big chunk of India's total economic strength.

5. Strict and hospitable: Think of SMEs as business superheroes. They can handle tough times and bounce back quickly. Their flexibility allows them to adapt and get through change, even when things get a little tough.

6. Team players: SMEs are not in isolation. They work closely with large companies and provide them with products or

services. This teamwork creates a mutually supportive system, which strengthens the overall economy.

We can say that SMEs are not just businesses; they are like the heartbeat that keeps the economy alive and beating, SME's are important not only because of their numbers but also because of the positive impact they have on people's lives, on local communities as not every business is Large Cap but once every large cap share was a Small cap or SME.

Explanation of the purpose and potential benefits of investing in SME stocks

Let's understand the objectives of investing in SME stocks, but before getting to the points lets go back to 1970's when a company named *Reliance* just started off and now in 2024 it is one of the biggest companies in India, so by investing in SME's we get a chance to grow with the company with its ups and downs both, and this is the right and easiest way to do it, let understand the objectives now:

1. Supporting Development: - When you invest in SMEs, you are basically supporting the growth of small businesses. Your money is a vote of confidence, helping these businesses expand, creating more jobs and supporting the economy.

2. Innovation Capital:- Small businesses are often centers of innovation. Investing in their portfolios provides them with the

capital they need to develop new products, services, or technologies that can ultimately change the game.

3. Promotion of entrepreneurship: - Investing in SMEs is one way to boost business growth. You support the dreams and ideas of entrepreneurs who have dared to start something on their own. This support can be a driving force for many people to take a leap into entrepreneurship.

4. Diversifying Your Portfolio: - SMEs can add diversification to your investment portfolio. While large companies make solid investments, small and medium-sized companies have the potential for rapid growth, and can provide exceptional returns on investment.

Potential advantages of investing in SME stocks:

1. High growth potential: - Smaller businesses tend to have more room to grow than older larger companies. If you choose the right SMEs, you can benefit greatly from the expansion of these services.

2. Early Application Opportunities: - Investing in SMEs can provide opportunities for early entry into potentially successful businesses. Landing on a company with strong growth prospects can be lucrative.

3.Innovation and Agility: SMEs are known for their innovation and agility. They can adapt quickly to market changes and introduce new ideas and products faster than larger companies. Investing in such companies shows that you are part of that dynamic and creative environment.

4.Contributed work: Your investments in SMEs can indirectly contribute to job creation. As these industries grow, they often employ more people, reducing unemployment and strengthening local economies.

5.Community Impact: Investment in SMEs can have a positive impact on local communities. Many SMEs operate on a small scale and are closely connected to their communities, so your investment can make a difference close to home.

Look investing always comes with risk, the potential benefits of investing in SMEs extend beyond financial returns. It's a way to diversify your investments and actively participate in the growth and success of small businesses. Just remember that like any investment, we have to do thorough research and understanding before making a decision.

Types of Companies Based on Size Market Cap Categories: Small, Mid, and Large:

In our Indian stock market, companies are categorized based on their market capitalization, which is the total market value of a company's outstanding shares.

This classification helps us to understand the size of a company.

Let's see how the three are classified numerically and how we can determine if a company is sme, small, mid, or large.

How to classify a company based on market capitalization?

Large Cap
Companies with a market cap of ₹20,000 crore or more, like Reliance Industries.

Mid Cap
Companies with a market cap between ₹5,000 crore and ₹20,000 crore, like Castrol India.

Small Cap/SME
Companies with a market cap less than ₹5,000 crore, often below ₹1,000 crore, like Shera Energy.

Hidden Wealth in SME Stocks
By
CA ANSHUL KARWA

1. Large Cap Companies:

- These are the top companies when ranked by market capitalization.

- Market Cap Range: These companies have a market cap of ₹20,000 crore or more.

- Example: Reliance Industries, Tata Motors

2. Mid-Cap Companies:

- Market Cap Range: In between ₹5,000 crore and ₹20,000 crore

- Example: Castrol India, Raymond

3. Small-Cap and SME Companies:

- Market Cap Range: Less than ₹5,000 crore. SME companies are mostly (not all) below ₹1,000 crore.

- Example: Shera Energy, KLL

> An investment in knowledge pays the best interest.

Benjamin Franklin

HIDDEN WEALTH IN SME STOCKS
BY
CA ANSHUL KARWA

Chapter 2: Introduction to the stock market and how it functions

Let's start with the basics, especially if you're new to this. If you're already familiar with this you can skip it. I'll explain things in simple terms so that you can easily grasp the concepts.

1. What is a Stock Market?
   Stock market is like a big market where people buy and sell shares of companies. Shares represent shares in a company, and if you own shares, you become a shareholder or shareholder of that company. Stock market is where these shares are bought and sold.

2. Players in the stock market:
   - Companies: Shares are sold to raise funds for various purposes such as expansion of the business, creation of new products, repayment of debt.

- Investors: These are individuals or institutions (such as mutual funds or pension funds) that buy corporate shares. They become shareholders and hope that the value of these shares will increase over time. - Brokers - These are like intermediaries who facilitate the buying and selling of shares. They're working on behalf of investors.

3. Treasury: Securities are traded on exchanges similar to an organized stock exchange market. For example, India has the National Stock Exchange (NSE) and the Bombay Stock Exchange (BSE). These exchanges provide a means of buying and selling shares.

4. How it works: - Listing: Companies that want to sell their shares to the public go through a process called an initial public offering (IPO). This

happens when a company lists its shares on the stock exchange for the first time.

- Buying and selling: After registration, investors can buy and sell these shares on the stock exchange. The price of a share is determined by the laws of supply and demand

– if more people want to buy the stock (demand) then the price goes up, if more people want to sell it (supply) then the price to the ground

- Stock indices: These are like indicators of the performance of the stock market as a whole or a particular sector. For example, in India you may have heard of the Nifty 50 or the Sensex these are indices that give an idea of how the stock market is doing.

5. Risks and Rewards:

   There are risks and rewards in investing. Prices can rise, generating income (rewards) for investors, but they can also fall, generating losses (risk). We have to understand the balance between risk and reward if you're investing in the stock market.

   In short, a stock market is a place where stocks in companies are bought and sold. It is a dynamic environment in which share prices can change based on a variety of factors, providing opportunities for individuals and organizations to participate in business development.

Let's learn some key terms and concepts regarding the stock market. We'll cover everything from stocks and SME IPOs to market capitalization and more:

1. Stock: - A stock, also known as a share or equity, represents ownership in a company. When you own a stock, you have a stake in the company. These stocks are bought and sold on stock exchanges.

2. SME IPOs (Initial Public Offerings): - SME IPOs are when a Small and Medium Enterprise (SME) first offers its shares to the public to raise capital. This allows investors to purchase shares in the company.

3. Market Capitalization (Market Cap):
   - Market capitalization refers to the total value of a company's outstanding shares of stock. This is determined by multiplying the current stock price by the number of shares.

4. Bull Market:
   A bull market is a length while inventory costs are growing, and investor confidence is excessive. It's characterised via optimism, improved buying interest, and an average effective economic outlook. This market is often liked by every investor.

Favorable for investors

Positive outlook

Optimism prevails

Strategic for traders

Negative outlook

Pessimism dominates

Bull Market

Bear Market

Compare market sentiments and strategies.

Hidden Wealth in SME Stocks
By
CA ANSHUL KARWA

5. Bear Market:

A endure marketplace is the other or opposite of a bull marketplace. It's a duration while stock expenses are falling, and investor confidence is low. Bear markets are related to pessimism and a commonly poor economic outlook. This market creates panic among investors and traders and is often not liked by investors but gives a chance to invest in good companies for long term. This market usually is good for traders who have short positions.

Bull market creates stupid investors, stupid investors create bear market, bear market creates smart investors and smart investors again create bull market.

-

Vijay Kedia

6. Dividends:
Dividends are a part of a organisation's income disbursed to its shareholders. Companies that pay dividends frequently achieve this as a manner to percentage earnings and entice traders.

7. Blue-Chip Stocks:
    Blue-chip shares are shares of big, nicely-established, and financially stable organizations. They are taken into consideration less volatile than stocks of smaller companies and are frequently part of essential stock indices.

8. Diversification:
    Diversification is like not putting all your eggs in one basket when it comes to investing. Instead of putting all your money into just one thing, you spread it out into different things, like stocks, bonds, real estate, and so on. This helps lower the risk of losing a lot of money if one investment doesn't do well, because the gains from other investments can help balance things out.

9. Earnings Per Share (EPS):
   Earnings consistent with proportion is a economic metric that represents the portion of a employer's profit allotted to every high-quality share of common inventory. It's a key indicator of a corporation's profitability.

10. Liquidity:
    Liquidity refers to how effortlessly an asset, like a stock, may be bought or bought in the market without affecting its rate. Highly liquid belongings may be quick bought or offered with minimal impact on their fee.

Now that we have understood the above phrases, now we can navigate the stock market effectively and make knowledgeable investment selections, especially whilst dealing with SME.

How stock prices are determined?

Stock costs are determined via the forces of deliver and call for inside the economic markets. The primary principle is that the fee of an inventory is prompted with the aid of how an awful lot buyers are inclined to pay for it (demand) and how much inventory is to be had for sale (deliver). Here's a simplified explanation with an example:

Supply and Demand:

When extra humans want to shop for a inventory than promote it, the call for increases, leading to a potential rise in its price.

Conversely, when more people want to sell a stock than purchase it, the deliver will increase, in all likelihood inflicting the inventory price to fall.

Market Orders and Limit Orders:

Investor's location orders to shop for or sell shares. Market orders are achieved at the modern-day marketplace charge, while restriction orders are set at a selected charge.

If the excellent to be had promote order suits a consumer's marketplace order, a transaction takes place at that fee.

Example:

IRCTC (Indian Railway Catering and Tourism Corporation) has shares listed on the stock exchange. The current market price is Rs 750 per share.

If many investors suddenly want to buy IRCTC shares, the demand increases. Sellers may start asking for a higher price, say Rs 755 per share.

As buyers are willing to pay more, the stock price can rise to Rs 755 if the highest bid matches a seller's asking price. For example, let's consider two individuals: Devashish (the buyer) and Kamal (the seller). If Devashish wishes to purchase IRCTC at Rs 750, but Kamal insists on selling it at Rs 755, the transaction cannot occur. Either Devashish must increase his offer price, or Kamal must decrease his asking price to align, allowing the transaction to proceed.

Market Sentiment and News:

News, events, and marketplace sentiment can impact deliver and call for.

Positive news approximately a corporation, such as sturdy profits, may growth call for and pressure up the inventory charge.

Negative information, alternatively, can cause improved selling and a capacity drop in stock prices.

For example, let's say Payal wants to sell her shares of a company to Mahesh. If Payal tells Mahesh that the company just announced record-breaking profits for the quarter, Mahesh might be eager to buy the shares at the current market price or even at a higher price because he expects the value of the stock to increase further. This positive news about the company's performance increases Mahesh's interest in buying the shares, and he might agree to Payal's asking price without much negotiation.

On the other hand, if Payal tells Mahesh that the company is facing a lawsuit for environmental damages, Mahesh might become hesitant about buying the shares. This negative news about the company's legal troubles could lead Mahesh to reconsider his decision to buy the shares, and he might either decide not to buy them at all or offer a lower price because he perceives higher risk associated with the investment.

Market Makers:

In active markets, there are often intermediaries known as marketplace makers. They facilitate buying and selling through buying and promoting shares at publicly quoted costs.

Market makers help hold liquidity and make sure that there is a continuous fluctuation of buying and selling in the market.

Imagine Shubham wants to buy shares of a company, and Tushita wants to sell some of her shares of the same company. In this scenario, they both approach the market, where market makers play a crucial role.

When Shubham places an order to buy shares, the market maker steps in and offers to sell shares to Shubham at a publicly quoted price, ensuring that Shubham can execute his trade immediately without having to wait for a seller like Tushita to appear. Similarly, when Tushita decides to sell her shares, the market maker is ready to buy them at the quoted price, providing liquidity to Tushita without her needing to find a buyer like Shubham right away.

By continuously offering to buy and sell shares at quoted prices, the market maker helps maintain a smooth flow of trading activity in the market. This ensures that both Shubham and Tushita can easily buy or sell shares whenever they want, contributing to overall market liquidity.

Discussion on the potential risks and rewards associated with SME stocks

Potential Rewards:

High Growth Potential:

Example: Imagine making an investment in a tech startup that develops revolutionary software program. If the employer effectively taps right into a growing market, its price and your funding could soar.

Undervalued Opportunities:

Example: A small manufacturing employer can be undervalued as compared to its large counterparts. If it expands its market share or introduces cost-effective manufacturing strategies, the inventory could see substantial appreciation.

Innovative and Niche Markets:

Example: Investing in a biotech SME focused on a gap healing vicinity. If their studies ends in a leap forward drug or treatment, the business enterprise's value and your investment could see good sized gains.

Potential for Mergers and Acquisitions (M&A)

Example: An SME with unique technology might attract the interest of a larger company looking to acquire innovative assets. Shareholders in the SME could benefit from a higher price paid during the purchase.

Potential Risks

Market Volatility:

Example: A surprising monetary downturn can effect SMEs appreciably, leading to reduced customer spending and lower revenues for the agency.

Limited Resources and Financial Stability:

Example: SMEs would possibly face demanding situations in securing funding all through hard financial situations, impacting their ability to extend or meet monetary obligations.

Operational Risks:

Example: A manufacturing SME closely dependent on a unmarried supplier for uncooked substances would possibly face disruptions if that supplier encounters problems, affecting manufacturing and economic performance.

Lack of Liquidity:

Example: SME stocks may have decrease buying and selling volumes compared to large corporations. If you need to sell shares fast, the shortage of liquidity can result in a decrease-than-expected sale price.

Regulatory and Compliance Challenges:

Example: Changes in guidelines can pose challenges for SMEs, mainly if compliance calls for big investments. Failure to conform may also cause monetary penalties or operational disruptions.

If you think compliance is expensive, Try non-compliance

-

Paul McNulty

Non-compliance leads to higher costs and legal risks.

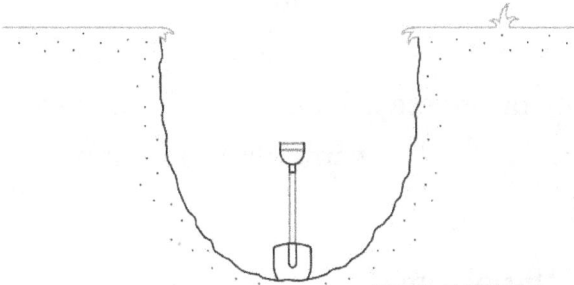

Hidden Wealth in SME Stocks
By
CA ANSHUL KARWA

Limited Analyst Coverage:

Example: SMEs often get hold of much less attention from monetary analysts for example Zee business or CNBC rarely discuss about SME shares, making it challenging for investors to get entry to complete information and insights, doubtlessly main to much less informed funding selections.

For example, Dhruv, Shubham, and Akshat are all entrepreneurs running their own small businesses. Each of them faces various risks that come with operating an SME.

For **Dhruv**, market volatility poses a significant risk. He runs a small electronics store, and sudden changes in consumer preferences or economic conditions can impact his sales dramatically. For example, if a new competitor enters the market with lower-priced electronics, Dhruv may struggle to compete and see a drop in his revenue.

Shubham's business, a small manufacturing unit, faces challenges related to limited resources and financial stability. He often struggles to secure enough funds to expand his operations or invest in new equipment. Without access to sufficient capital, Shubham finds it difficult to grow his business and stay competitive in the market.

Akshat operates a small restaurant, facing operational risks on a daily basis. From supply chain disruptions to equipment failures, any unexpected event can disrupt his business operations and lead to financial losses. For instance, if there's a sudden shortage of ingredients due to transportation issues, Akshat may have to temporarily close his restaurant, resulting in lost revenue.

Additionally, all three entrepreneurs face the risk of lack of liquidity, especially during slow business periods or emergencies. If Dhruv, Shubham, or Akshat encounter unexpected expenses or need to access funds quickly, they may struggle to convert their assets into cash, impacting their ability to cover expenses or seize growth opportunities.

Furthermore, the regulatory and compliance challenges adds another layer of risk for Dhruv, Shubham, and Akshat. They must ensure that their businesses comply with various laws and regulations related to taxation, health and safety standards, and employment practices. Any non-compliance could result in penalties or legal consequences, further straining their financial resources.

Thus as a result, Dhruv, Shubham, and Akshat face a range of risks inherent to operating SMEs, including market volatility, limited resources and financial stability, operational challenges, lack of liquidity, and regulatory compliance issues.

So, we as an investor in SME stocks should cautiously verify the related risks and rewards, thinking about elements which include the organisation's financial health, industry dynamics, and the wider economic surroundings. Diversification and thorough due diligence are critical while thinking about investments in smaller businesses, we'll understand about diversification later in this book.

Factors influencing stock prices in the SME segment

Earnings and Financial Performance:

Definition: The monetary health and performance of a commercial enterprise, such as revenue boom, profitability, and earnings in keeping with percentage.

Example: If a lemonade stand always makes more money every month, buyers is probably extra inclined to shop for stocks in that small enterprise.

Market Sentiment:

Definition: Investor perceptions and sentiments approximately a specific market or enterprise.

Example: If everybody for your community loves shopping for cookies from a nearby bakery, the fine sentiment may encourage extra people to make investments in the bakery's stock.

Industry Trends:

Definition: The usual direction wherein an enterprise is heading, impacting the performance of groups inside it.

Example: If all the children on your faculty start playing a new video game, the enterprise that makes that sport can also see multiplied income and a better stock rate.

Macroeconomic Factors:

Definition: Economic indicators inclusive of hobby prices, inflation, and GDP growth that could impact businesses.

Example: If more humans in your city get jobs, they could have extra money to spend on goods and services, probably reaping benefits nearby corporations and their stocks.

Competitive Landscape:

Definition: The shape and dynamics of competition in a particular market.

Example: If a small toy store is the handiest one on the town, it would have a aggressive advantage, attracting more clients and probably boosting its inventory price.

Company News and Developments:

Definition: Information and events associated with a business enterprise which can affect its overall performance.

Example: Imagine Baskin-Robbins, a popular ice cream company, introduces a new flavor called "Rainbow Delight." This flavor quickly becomes a hit among customers, with people loving its colorful appearance and delicious taste.

As news spreads about the popularity of "Rainbow Delight," more customers flock to Baskin-Robbins stores to try it out. The increased demand for this new flavor leads to higher sales for the company, boosting its overall performance.

In response to the positive reception of "Rainbow Delight," investors also show confidence in Baskin-Robbins, causing the company's stock price to rise. This increase in stock price reflects the market's belief that Baskin-Robbins is successfully meeting consumer preferences and driving growth through innovative products like "Rainbow Delight."

In this example, the introduction of a new ice cream flavor (Rainbow Delight) by Baskin-Robbins generates positive news and events that contribute to the company's overall performance by attracting more customers and potentially increasing its stock price.

Market Liquidity:

Definition: The ease with which belongings (like shares) may be sold or offered within the market.

Investor Perception and Behaviour:

Definition: How investors perceive and react to market statistics and traits.

Example: Imagine Saily and Himani are both investors in a streaming service company for e.g. Netflix. They hear from their friends and see on social media that the streaming service has acquired the rights to stream "Game of Thrones," one of the most popular and highly acclaimed TV series of all time. People are buzzing with excitement, saying they can't wait to watch it again or for the first time.

Saily and Himani start thinking that if everyone else is so hyped about "Game of Thrones" coming to their streaming service, more people will want to subscribe to watch it. This could lead to a surge in subscriptions and revenue for the streaming service, potentially boosting its stock price. So, they might decide to buy shares of the streaming service company, hoping to profit from the increased demand for its content due to "Game of Thrones."

In this example, investor perception and behaviour are influenced by the anticipation surrounding the arrival of "Game of Thrones" on the streaming service. Saily and Himani, like other investors, are likely to react to this positive sentiment by purchasing shares of the streaming service company, expecting the popularity of "Game of Thrones" to drive up its stock price.

Technological Advances:

Definition: Innovations and upgrades in era that can impact commercial enterprise operations.

Example: Gurdeep, the owner of a transport business, decides to invest in GPS tracking systems and fleet management software. By equipping his vehicles with this technology, Gurdeep can efficiently monitor their routes, optimize fuel consumption, and improve delivery timelines. As a result, his transport business becomes more competitive and reliable, attracting more clients and potentially increasing the company's valuation.

Management Quality:

Definition: The competence and effectiveness of a agency's management.

Example: Kamal, a bedsheets manufacturer, demonstrates how the quality of management can profoundly impact a business. With his meticulous attention to detail and proactive problem-solving abilities, Kamal ensures smooth operations within his company. For instance, his efficient management of production processes and timely resolution of issues result in high-quality bedsheets and satisfied customers. Kamal's effective leadership not only maintains his company's reputation but also drives its growth and success in the market.

Access to Capital:

Definition: The potential of a organisation to reap funding for growth or operations.

Example:

Imagine Devashish, who runs a business manufacturing agarbattis(incense sticks), wants to expand his operations. He decides to approach a local bank for a loan to help him grow. Impressed by Devashish's business plan and the potential for growth in the agarbatti market, the bank approves his loan application without difficulty.

With the loan, Devashish invests in purchasing additional machinery and raw materials to increase his production capacity. As a result, he is able to produce more agarbattis and fulfill larger orders from retailers and wholesalers. The increased production leads to higher sales and attracts more customers to his business.

The expanded operations and improved efficiency contribute to the growth of Devashish's agarbatti manufacturing business. This growth not only boosts his revenue but also enhances the reputation of his brand in the market.

So, by using different financial resources effectively, Devashish is able to enhance his business and potentially increase its profitability and market share in the agarbatti industry.

> "Respect the market. Have an open mind. Know what to stake. Know when to take a loss. Be responsible.

Rakesh Jhunjhunwala

HIDDEN WEALTH IN SME STOCKS
BY
CA ANSHUL KARWA

Chapter 3:
Real life case studies of successful SME stocks

Let's discuss couple of real-life examples of successful Small and Medium-sized Enterprises (SMEs) listing in India:

1. Kesar India Limited (BSE: KESAR)
    -Industry: Construction

    -Success Story: Guess what happened in the stock market from July 2022 to Feb 2024? This SME stock, starting at Rs 100, decided to go on a crazy rollercoaster ride and reached a whopping Rs 1700! Yep, you heard it right—talk about a wild 1.5-year journey.

    So, picture this: From Rs 170 to almost Rs 100 and then rising to Rs 3072 – talk about a financial rollercoaster that keeps on giving! Investors who got in at the Rs 100 or even at IPO price mark are probably doing a happy dance right about now.

What's behind this stock market magic? Well, it could be a mix of smart business moves, some clever financial moves, and a dash of good old market hype. Maybe the company aced its game with killer financial reports, made some genius decisions, or simply became the talk of the town.

Whatever it is, one thing's for sure, those who bet on this stock during this time frame hit the jackpot. This story isn't just about numbers on a screen, it's a tale of how the stock market can be this crazy, unpredictable adventure.

For those who caught wind of the rising star in time, it's not just about making money, it's about being part of a thrilling ride where Rs 100 turned into a jaw-dropping Rs 3072 in just a blink. Talk about turning small change into a jackpot!

It's more than 2972% increase from the bottom(Rs 100).

Check the on next page:

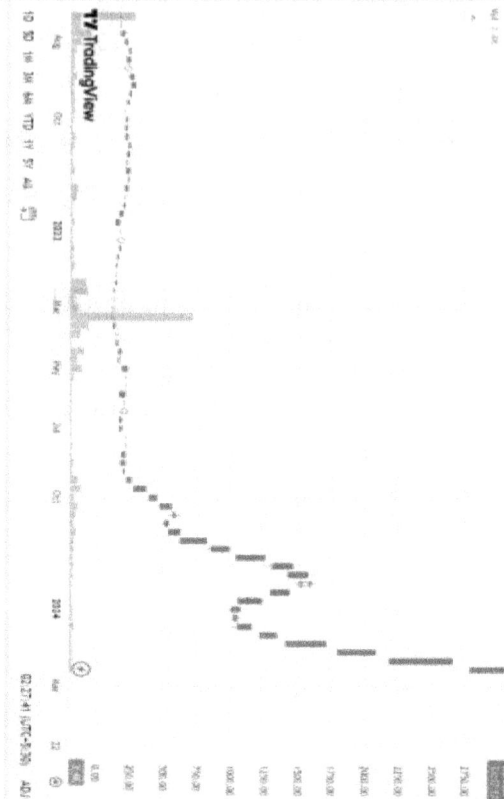

2. Concord Control Systems Limited(BSE):

   - Industry: Retail - Engineering - Industrial Equipments

   - Success Story - Concord Control Systems Ltd. has quite the story to tell. Starting at an IPO price of Rs 55, the company's stock soared to an impressive Rs 1000 in less than a year. That's a 1700% increase!

This rapid rise is a testament to the company's smart moves and how it captured the market's attention. Investors who got in early saw their investments skyrocket, making Concord Control Systems Ltd. a standout success in the world of SME stocks.

This journey from Rs 55 to Rs 1000 in such a short time is a valuable lesson for anyone interested in stocks. It shows that, even in the ever-changing world of finance, there are opportunities for substantial growth. Concord Control Systems Ltd.'s success is a reminder that sometimes, simplicity can lead to incredible results in the stock market.

3. Krishna Defence and Allied Industries Limited (NSE):

- Industry: Defence

- Success Story: Krishna Defence and Allied Industries Limited, since its IPO debut in 2022, has been on a noteworthy journey in the stock market. Starting at Rs 55, the stock saw a substantial increase, reaching a peak at Rs 400. This impressive climb represents a significant surge of over 627%, showcasing the stock's substantial growth within a relatively short period.

The shift from a low of Rs 55 to a high of Rs 400 not only highlights the stock's responsiveness to market changes but also tells a compelling story of investment potential. Investors who recognized and took advantage of this upward trend likely experienced significant returns, positioning Krishna Defence and Allied Industries Limited as a compelling player in the world of stock market successes.

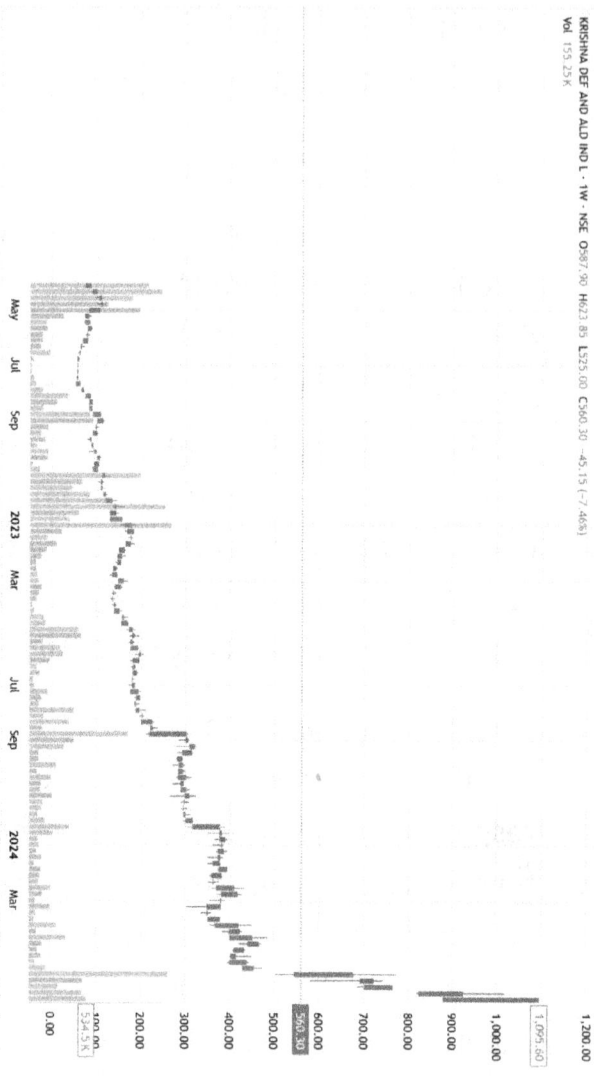

KRISHNA DEF AND ALD IND L · 1W · NSE O587.90 H623.85 L525.00 C560.30 −45.15 (−7.46%)
Vol 155.25K

1,095.60

560.30

100.00
534.5 K

TradingView

4. Suratwwala Business Group Ltd.(NSE)

- Industry: Construction - Real Estate

- Success Story: Suratwwala Business Group Ltd has seen a significant change since it first started with an IPO price of Rs 15. Now, the Current Market Price (CMP) is at an impressive 763, showing a substantial increase. This amounts to a remarkable surge of over 4953% till 2024, reflecting substantial growth over its journey.

Calculating this percentage increase on a yearly basis gives us an approximate yearly growth rate of around 618% per year. This highlights the consistent upward trend and significant value created for investors in Suratwwala Business Group Ltd. This impressive performance makes the company stand out in the world of the stock market.

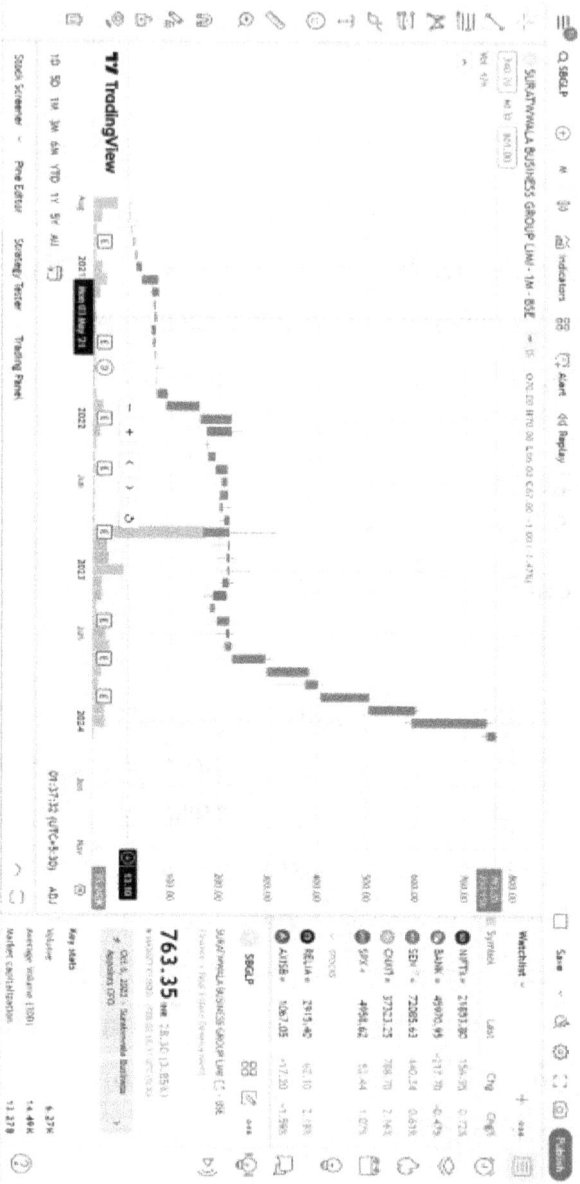

5. Vasa Denticity Ltd.(NSE):

- Industry: Trading

- Success Story: Vasa Denticity Ltd. has had quite a journey since it launched its IPO in June 2023 at a price of 128. The stock didn't just stop there; it went on to hit a high of 720 and more in just a few months. This quick and substantial growth shows how lively the stock market can be. If we look at the numbers, the return from the IPO price of 128 to the high of 720 is quite impressive. Investors saw their money grow by over 462% during this period, highlighting the significant potential for making gains with Vasa Denticity Ltd.

This success story again shines a light on the SME sector, proving it can be a promising avenue for making money. The quick rise of Vasa Denticity Ltd. is a glimpse into how the stock market is changing, offering new opportunities for wealth creation.

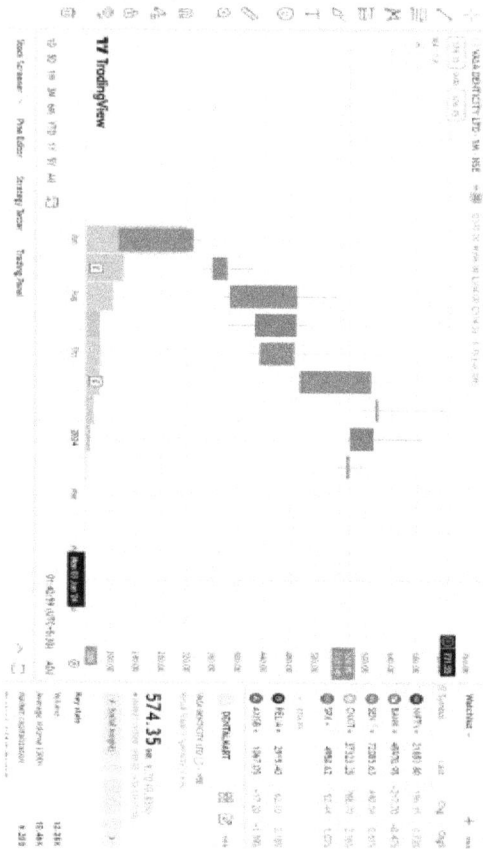

6. Isolation Energy Limited (BSE)

- Industry: Electronics Components

- Success Story: Insolation Energy Ltd. has shown remarkable growth, moving from Rs 75 to Rs 1200 in less than two years. This SME stock has truly shone brightly, proving to be a valuable investment.

The journey from Rs 75 to Rs 1200 is quite impressive, highlighting the stock's substantial increase in value. This success story indicates the potential for significant returns within a relatively short timeframe.

Insolation Energy Ltd. stands out as a gem in the SME sector, showcasing the exciting possibilities that exist for investors. This swift rise in value is a testament to the evolving landscape of the stock market, offering opportunities for wealth creation.

TV TradingView

1D 5D 1M 3M 6M YTD 1Y 5Y All

2023   May   Sep   2024

1234.95

INSOLATION ENERGY LIMITED · BSE

Key RSVD

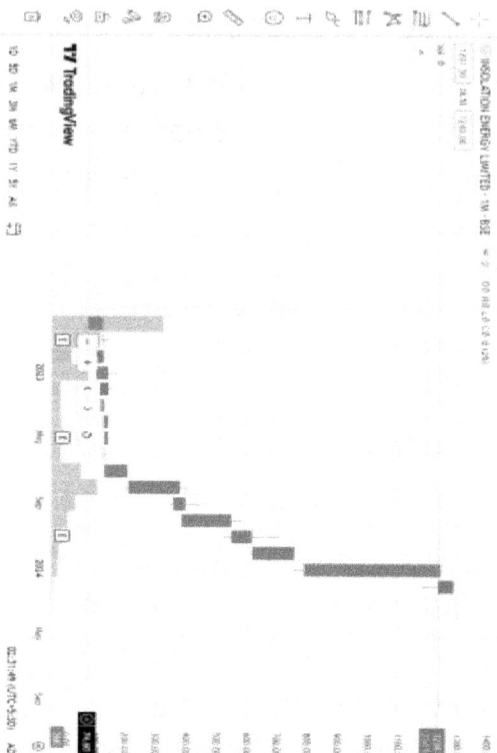

Stock Screener · Pine Editor   Screening / Tester   Trading Panel

Story From SME to Mainboard-

Gensol Engineering Limited (BSE: GENSOL)

- **Industry:** Renewable Energy & Engineering Services

- **Success Story:** Gensol Engineering, initially listed on the SME platform, has emerged as a key player in the renewable energy sector, specializing in solar EPC (Engineering, Procurement, and Construction) services. Over time, the company expanded its operations, venturing into electric vehicle manufacturing and strengthening its position in the clean energy ecosystem.

Gensol Engineering began its journey on the SME platform with an initial stock price of approximately Rs 83. With consistent growth, strategic expansion, and increasing demand for solar power solutions, the company's stock surged to an impressive Rs 1,376. Its transition from an SME to a well-established enterprise showcases its strong fundamentals, innovation-driven approach, and growing investor confidence.

The remarkable rise in its stock price reflects Gensol's commitment to sustainable solutions and its ability to capitalize on India's renewable energy boom. The company's growth from a small SME to a strong industry player is an inspiration for small businesses aiming for big success.

Waaree Renewable Technologies Limited (BSE: WAAREERTL)

- **Industry:** Renewable Energy - Solar Modules & EPC

- **Success Story:** Waaree Renewable Technologies, a subsidiary of the renowned Waaree Group, made its debut on the SME platform and quickly gained recognition for its contribution to the solar energy sector. The company specializes in solar module manufacturing and EPC services, catering to India's growing demand for renewable energy solutions.

When it was first listed in 2019, Waaree Renewable's stock was priced at **Rs 22**, making it an attractive investment opportunity for early backers. With the increasing focus on clean energy and government initiatives promoting solar adoption, the stock witnessed an extraordinary surge, reaching an all-time high of **Rs 3,037**. This growth trajectory underscores the company's robust business model, strong execution capabilities, and the massive potential of the renewable energy sector in India.

Waaree Renewable Technologies' success exemplifies how an SME with a strong vision and execution strategy can scale rapidly and create significant value for investors. Its journey from a modest beginning to becoming a market leader highlights the opportunities available in India's clean energy transition and the potential for SMEs to evolve into industry giants.

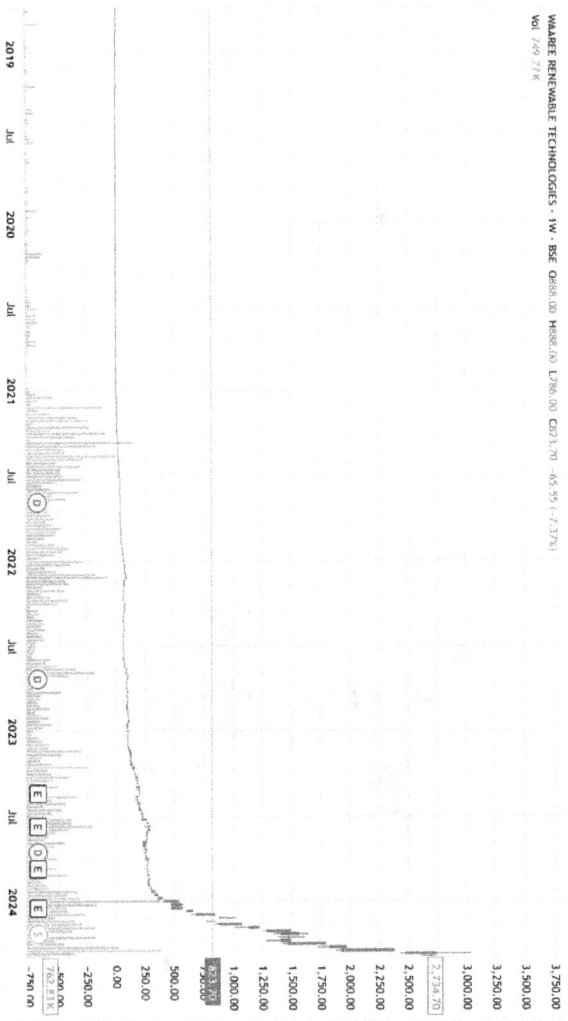

WAAREE RENEWABLE TECHNOLOGIES · 1W · BSE O688.00 H688.00 L786.00 C823.70 −65.55 (−7.37%)
Vol 749.77K

2,734.70

823.70
782.31%

3,750.00
3,500.00
3,250.00
3,000.00
2,750.00
2,500.00
2,250.00
2,000.00
1,750.00
1,500.00
1,250.00
1,000.00
750.00
500.00
250.00
0.00
-250.00
-500.00
-750.00

2019 Jul 2020 Jul 2021 Jul 2022 Jul 2023 Jul 2024

TradingView

75

> **Stock markets are always right. Never time the market.**
>
> Rakesh Jhunjhunwala

HIDDEN WEALTH IN SME STOCKS
BY
CA ANSHUL KARWA

Chapter 4: IPOs and the SME Segment

Understanding Initial Public Offerings (IPOs) and their significance

Let's explore Small and Medium Enterprises (SME) Initial Public Offerings (IPOs) and understand their significance.

When a small or medium-sized enterprise (SME) decides to go public, it means they are opening their doors to public investment through an Initial Public Offering or IPO. Now, why is this a big deal?

Firstly, it's a way for these smaller companies to raise capital from a broader group of investors. By doing so, they can fund expansions, improve infrastructure, or fuel various business initiatives.

Secondly, SME IPOs provide an opportunity for investors to be a part of the growth story of these smaller businesses. It's like getting a backstage pass to the early days of a potentially successful venture.

Furthermore, SME IPOs contribute to the overall vibrancy of the stock market. They introduce a diverse range of companies, fostering innovation and competition.

On the flip side, for investors, participating in SME IPOs provides a unique opportunity. It's like getting a sneak peek into the early chapters of a potentially successful business story. Just like we read about Gensol Engineering and Waaree Renewable Technologies in our real life examples, investing in an SME at this stage can be rewarding if the company manages to navigate the market effectively and grow. They introduce a variety of businesses, each with its unique strengths and ideas. This diversity creates innovation and healthy competition, making the business landscape more vibrant.

In simpler terms, SME IPOs are like the entrance ticket to a show where both the company and investors can benefit.

It's a win-win situation, bringing new opportunities and energy to the business world and returns to the investors.

When a SME company in India chooses to sell its shares to the public, it starts on a systematic journey to enter the stock market, it is not a overnight task. Lets discuss an easy to understand overview of how SMEs goes Public(IPO) in India.

1. Preparation of Mindset and process:

- The SME IPO process starts from the IPO process by engaging with, ipo advisors, financial experts including Chartered Accountants, legal advisors, and underwriters to prepare for the public offering.

- The company must ensure compliance with regulatory requirements and financial transparency.

2. Appointment of Intermediaries:

- The SME appoints various intermediaries, including underwriters, merchant bankers, and legal advisors, to guide them through the IPO process.

3. Due Diligence:

- A thorough due diligence process is conducted to verify the company's financial health, compliance, and governance practices by merchant bankers and their team of experts.

4. Drafting the Red Herring Prospectus (RHP):

- The company, with the help of merchant bankers and underwriters, prepares the Red Herring Prospectus, which provides key information about the company, its operations, financials, and the IPO.

5. Submission to Regulatory Authorities:

- The SME submits the RHP to regulatory authorities such as the , NSE Emerge or BSE and Securities and Exchange Board of India (SEBI) for approval.

6. Roadshow:

- The company and its underwriters conduct a roadshow to generate interest among potential investors including Pre-IPO selling of shares and searching for Anchor Investor. This involves presentations and interactions with institutional and retail investors.

7. Price Discovery:

- The company, along with merchant bankers and underwriters, determines the issue price through a book-building process or fixed price method.

8. Allotment and Listing:

- The shares are allotted to investors, and the SME's stock is listed on the stock exchanges.

9. Post-IPO Compliance:

- The SME must adhere to post-IPO compliance requirements, including regular financial reporting, disclosure, and compliance with SEBI regulations.

10. Trading Commencement:

- The SME's shares commence trading on the stock exchanges either BSE or NSE, allowing investors or shareholders to buy and sell the company's stocks.

The above process explained is a very basic process just to give a basic idea of how the process goes on.

The process of SME IPO takes from around minimum 3 months to upto 2 years depending upon the condition and restatement required by SEBI, exchanges and other regulatory requirements.

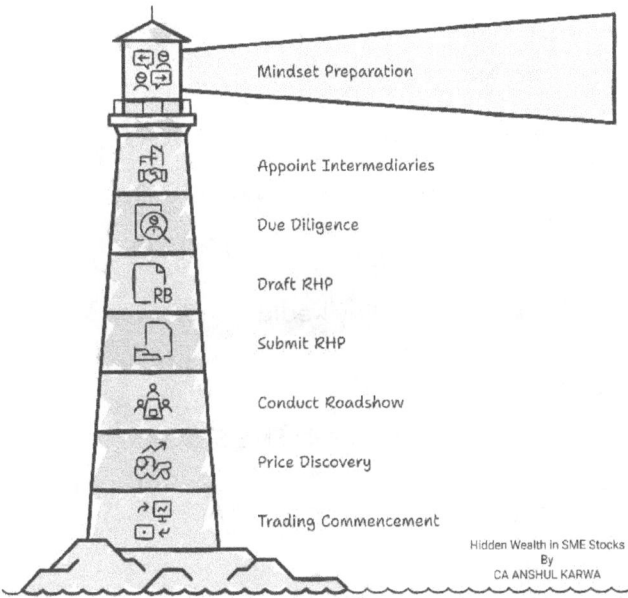

Steps to SME IPO in India

Mindset Preparation

Appoint Intermediaries

Due Diligence

Draft RHP

Submit RHP

Conduct Roadshow

Price Discovery

Trading Commencement

Hidden Wealth in SME Stocks
By
CA ANSHUL KARWA

> ## 3 qualities of a good investor: Knowledge, Courage & Patience.
>
> VIjay Kedia

HIDDEN WEALTH IN SME STOCKS
BY
CA ANSHUL KARWA

Chapter 5: How to Evaluate SME Stocks

Fundamental analysis for SME stocks

When we talk about fundamental analysis for SME stocks, it's essentially about understanding the core aspects that drive a company's value. Here's a practical way to look at it:

1. Company Finances:

Check out the company's financial statements – the balance sheet, income statement, and cash flow statement. These documents provide a snapshot of its financial health. Look for consistent revenue growth, manageable debt levels, and positive cash flow.

2. Market Position:

Consider the company's position in the market. Does it have a unique product or service? Is it gaining or losing market share? Understanding the competitive landscape helps assess the company's potential for future growth.

3. Management Team:

Evaluate the leadership. A competent and experienced management team is crucial. Look for a team that has a clear vision, strategic direction, and a track record of making sound business decisions.

4. Earnings Performance:

Dig into the company's earnings history. Steady and growing profits over time are a good sign. Consistency in earnings reflects a stable and well-managed business.

5. Industry Outlook:

Examine the industry the SME operates in. A strong industry outlook can positively impact the company's prospects. Conversely, challenges in the industry may pose risks.

6. Valuation:

Assess the stock's valuation. Compare its current price to earnings (P/E) ratio with industry averages. A stock that appears undervalued may present a buying opportunity.

The above are the main six aspects which we should assess while choosing a SME stock.

Let me show you how to practically do it with help of an example:

We'll take example of a SME stock named: Shera Energy Limited (NSE: Shera)

The company is listed on National Stock Exchange (NSE) is a SME company engaged in the business of manufacturing winding wires and strips made of non-ferrous metals primarily Copper and Aluminium.

Let's look at its P&L:

Profit & Loss

Consolidated Figures in Rs. Crores / View Standalone

	Mar 2020	Mar 2021	Mar 2022	Mar 2023	TTM
Sales +	425	433	524	696	797
Expenses +	398	398	490	658	750
Operating Profit	20	32	34	39	47
OPM %	7%	8%	6%	6%	6%
Other Income +	1	1	1	1	4
Interest	20	21	20	22	27
Depreciation	4	5	5	5	5
Profit before tax	6	7	10	13	18
Tax %	28%	26%	31%	27%	
Net Profit +	4	5	7	9	14
EPS in Rs	1.24	2.90	3.32	4.00	6.11

From the above image we can see that from March 2021 to March 2023 its Sales is consistently increasing year by year.

Now, lets check Net Profit, it is also increasing year by year, that means there's a consistent growth in the company.

Let's check the cash flow now:

	Mar 2020	Mar 2021	Mar 2022	Mar 2023
Cash from Operating Activity +	20	91	11	13
Cash from Investing Activity +	-4	3	6	1
Cash from Financing Activity +	-16	-37	-4	
Net Cash Flow	-0	8	-9	2

In March 2022, the company's cash flow was -3, which means it was negative. But by March 2023, things changed for the better, and the cash flow turned positive. This is good because it shows that the company's finances are improving. What's even better is that the money the company makes from its regular operations (like selling products or services) is now more than what it spends. This is really important because it means the company can cover its day-to-day expenses. So, with both the overall cash flow and the money from operations being positive in March 2023, it's a sign that the company is in better financial shape. This could attract new investors and make people think positively about the company's finances.

Let's check the ratios:

Ratios

Consolidated Figures in Rs. Crores | View Standalone

	Mar 2020	Mar 2021	Mar 2022	Mar 2023
Debtor Days	81	87	70	50
Inventory Days	81	100	108	93
Days Payable	69	107	84	83
Cash Conversion Cycle	58	59	68	60
Working Capital Days	63	75	71	87
ROCE %		16%	14%	17%

Debtor Days:

Decreasing debtor days (from 81 to 50) suggests the company is collecting payments from customers more quickly. This can positively impact cash flow, potentially boosting investor confidence.

Inventory Days:

A decrease in inventory days (from 100 to 93) indicates improved inventory management. This could lead to cost savings and better liquidity, potentially favoring the stock.

Days Payable:

A decrease in days payable (from 107 to 83) suggests the company is paying its suppliers more efficiently. While this can improve relationships, it's essential to ensure it doesn't negatively affect supplier relations.

Cash Conversion Cycle:

The cash conversion cycle, reflecting the time it takes to convert sales into cash, has seen a slight decrease. This can be perceived positively, indicating improved working capital management.

Working Capital Days:

The overall trend of decreasing working capital days (from 70 to 67) suggests more efficient utilization of working capital. This is generally seen as a positive sign.

Return on Capital Employed (ROCE):

ROCE has shown a consistent improvement (from 16% to 17%). A higher ROCE indicates effective utilization of capital, potentially attracting investors and positively influencing the stock price.

Let's check the Shareholding Pattern:

Shareholding Pattern

Promoters:

The promoters' shareholding has remained relatively stable, with a slight increase from 63.50% in March 2023 to 63.58% in September 2023. Promoters holding a majority stake can signify their commitment and confidence in the company.

Foreign Institutional Investors (FIIs):

The FIIs' shareholding has decreased significantly, dropping from 6.34% in March 2023 to 0.22% in September 2023. A substantial reduction in FII holding may raise questions about international investors' perception of the stock.

Domestic Institutional Investors (DIIs):

DIIs, while relatively minimal, have shown a slight increase from 0.00% to 0.09%. Though the percentage is low, any positive movement in DIIs' interest can be seen as a positive signal.

Public Shareholding:

Public shareholding has increased notably from 30.15% in March 2023 to 36.12% in September 2023. This suggests growing interest among retail and institutional investors, potentially contributing to increased liquidity in the stock.

Now here, upon closer examination, a red flag becomes evident as Foreign Institutional Investors (FIIs) have substantially reduced their stake. While the promoters are increasing their shareholding and Domestic Institutional Investors (DIIs) have also shown an uptick, the significant decrease in FII involvement raises concerns. This scenario could potentially pose a danger for the company. It's important to remain vigilant and consider the implications of these shifts in shareholding dynamics, as the reduced interest from FIIs may impact the overall market perception and stability of the stock.

Now let's check the balance sheet:

Balance Sheet					
Consolidated Figures in Rs. Crores / View Standalone					
	Mar 2019	Mar 2020	Mar 2021	Mar 2022	Sep 2022
Equity Capital	78	80	20	23	23
Reserves	19	41	42	95	71
Borrowings +	111	108	116	113	119
Other Liabilities +	109	126	140	111	198
Total Liabilities	277	294	325	375	411
Fixed Assets +	91	84	82	84	90
CWIP	2	4	3	2	3
Investments	0	0	0	0	0
Other Assets +	185	208	240	288	316
Total Assets	277	294	325	375	411

Analyzing the balance sheet provides insights into a company's financial health and resource allocation. Let's break down the key components:

1. Equity Capital:

- The equity capital has seen an increase from 20 to 23, indicating potential capital infusion or other corporate actions that expanded the company's ownership base.

2. Reserves:

- Reserves have consistently grown from 38 to 71. This signifies accumulated profits or retained earnings, reflecting the company's financial stability and capacity for reinvestment.

3. Borrowings:

- Borrowings have fluctuated but remained relatively stable, indicating prudent debt management. Monitoring borrowings is crucial to assess the company's leverage and debt service capability.

4. Other Liabilities:

- Other liabilities have steadily increased from 109 to 198. This category includes items like trade payables and provisions. A significant rise may warrant a closer look to understand the nature of these liabilities.

5. Total Liabilities:

- The total liabilities have grown from 277 to 411, showcasing the expansion of the company's financial obligations and commitments.

6. Fixed Assets and CWIP:

- Fixed assets and Capital Work in Progress (CWIP) have remained relatively stable, indicating a consistent level of investment in tangible assets and ongoing projects.

7. Investments:

- The balance sheet reflects no investments, suggesting the company has not deployed funds in financial instruments like stocks or securities.

8. Other Assets:

- Other assets have shown a consistent upward trend from 189 to 324, indicating potential diversification or expansion activities.

9. Total Assets:

- The total assets have increased from 277 to 411, showing the overall growth and expansion of the company.

10. Uniqueness of Company

Investing in a unique company means putting your money into a business that stands out from others. These companies usually have something special about them, like a product or service that nobody else offers. Choosing such a company can be smart because it often means they have loyal customers and might make more money. Plus, unique companies are often good at coming up with new ideas, which can keep them successful over time. When you invest in a unique company, you're also spreading out your investments, which can lower your risk. And sometimes, these special companies catch the eye of bigger companies who might want to buy them, which could mean a big payoff for investors like you. So, investing in unique companies can be a smart way to make your money grow.

Overall Assessment:

- The balance sheet reveals a company that has experienced growth and expansion, with increased equity capital, reserves, and total assets. The stability in fixed assets and borrowings suggests a balanced approach to financial management. However, the significant rise in other liabilities may be a red flag and require further scrutiny to ensure responsible financial practices.

Fundamental Analysis of SME Stocks

Industry Outlook
- Positive Outlook
- Challenges

Valuation
- Price to Earnings Ratio
- Undervalued Stocks

Company Finances
- Balance Sheet
- Income Statement
- Cash Flow Statement

Fundamental Analysis of SME Stocks

Market Position
- Unique Product/Service
- Market Share

Management Team
- Experience
- Track Record

Earnings Performance
- Steady Profits
- Growth Over Time

Now, lets check the PE Ratio of PEER's (competitor comparison):

Peer comparison

Sector: Non-Ferrous Metals   Industry: Mining / Minerals / Metals

S.No.	Name	CMP Rs.	P/E	Mar Cap Rs.Cr	Div Yld %	NP Qtr Rs.Cr.	Qtr Profit Var %	Sales Qtr Rs.Cr	Qtr Sales Var %	ROCE %
1.	Hindustan Zinc	376.20	18.13	158448.81	23.73	2678.00	-5.02	7316.00	7.00	54.36
2.	Hindustan Copper	351.10	60.37	20717.09	0.31	65.81	134.97	861.40	76.79	18.04
3.	Gravita India	884.15	36.33	6138.16	0.49	65.47	26.04	917.33	2.98	23.95
4.	Rajesh Exp.	430.33	46.33	8106.94	0.70	5.29	55.43	347.79	-1.45	16.78
5.	Shivalik Bimetal	581.55	43.47	3540.97	0.31	13.68	6.80	172.19	3.72	27.98
6.	Nav. Alloy...	148.90	43.54	3950.07	0.98	16.35	71.54	809.84	18.24	26.79
7.	Ramkrishna Alloy	516.05	35.09	1391.62	0.79	11.71	-9.58	586.40	14.04	17.09
8.	Shera Energy	177.18	33.20	403.58	0.00	5.20	51.11	206.12	34.79	16.83
	Madhav All Op.	393.54	27.28	1194.65	2.4	6.04	29.79	280.09	-9.34	17.52

Now here we see that Shera Energy presents a balanced financial profile with a moderate P/E ratio, reflecting a fair valuation in relation to its earnings. The company's market capitalization of Rs. 403.58 Cr. provides investors with a comprehensive snapshot of its overall market value. Shera Energy demonstrates a significant positive change in quarterly profits, with a noteworthy Qtr Profit Var % of 51.11%. The Return on Capital Employed (ROCE) at 16.83% suggests a moderate efficiency in utilizing capital.

In the overall assessment, Shera Energy's positive quarterly performance, mixed with a balanced P/E ratio and ROCE, indicates a favorable financial standing.

Final Verdict:

Considering Shera Energy's financial indicators, including the moderate P/E ratio, and Qtr Profit Var %, and a ROCE of 16.83%, the company exhibits positive financial aspects. However, the absence of dividends, as reflected in the 0.00% Dividend Yield, could impact income-oriented investors.

(Almost all SME's are in growth stage so they don't usually pay dividend)

Before deciding to invest at the current price, a thorough analysis of the Profit and Loss statement and cash flow statements is crucial, which we did and was positive.

While Shera Energy's current financial indicators are favorable, making an investment decision should be based on a risk tolerance, a stop loss and the broader market conditions. It's not a bad idea to buy Shera Energy Ltd for a long-term portfolio.

> Risk comes from not knowing what you're doing.

Warren Buffett

HIDDEN WEALTH IN SME STOCKS
BY
CA ANSHUL KARWA

Chapter 6: Building a Portfolio with SME Stocks

Diversification strategies for incorporating SME stocks in a portfolio

When you're building a portfolio, including SME (small and medium-sized enterprise) stocks can be a smart move, but it's important to think about diversification. Diversification means spreading your investments across different types of assets to reduce risk.

Let's discuss some easy diversification strategies for incorporating SME stocks in your portfolio:

1.Futuristic Sectors: Invest in SMEs operating in emerging and innovative industries. For example,

a) **Network People Services Technologies Ltd. (NPST):** Specializes in digital payment solutions and fintech services, catering to the growing demand for cashless transactions.

b) **Saakshi Medtech & Panels Ltd.:** Engages in manufacturing medical technology equipment, aligning with advancements in healthcare technology.

c) **Global Pet Industries Ltd.:** Focuses on producing eco-friendly PET products, contributing to sustainable packaging solutions.

2. Mix of Industries: Invest in SME stocks from various sectors such as IT, healthcare, consumer goods, and finance. For example, you could include stocks like Cool Caps Ltd. (Plastic caps), Asarfi Hospital Ltd. (healthcare), Kaushalya Logistics Limited (transport), and Shera Energy Ltd (Manufacturing).

2. Different Sizes of Companies in SME: Under SME stocks, include stocks from large, mid, and small sme companies. For example, you might invest in large SME company like Kesar India, mid-cap

companies like Cool Caps Ltd, and small SME stock like Arabian Petroleum.

3. Geographical Spread: Look for SME stocks from different regions in India. For instance, consider companies based in different states like Gujarat, Maharashtra, Karnataka, etc. For example, Cool Caps Ltd (based in West Bengal), Shera Energy Ltd (based in Rajasthan), and Asarfi Hospital Ltd (based in Jharkhand).

4. Asset Classes: Consider diversifying beyond stocks. You could invest in SMEs through mutual funds or exchange-traded funds (ETFs) that focus on SME stocks. For example, the SVL – SME Fund by SBI or Chanakya Fund Trust AIF which provides a platform for both Indian and foreign investors to pool their resources and invest in promising SMEs. Operating as a Category II AIF-SME Fund, Chanakya Fund focuses on unlisted securities of SMEs or those listed on SME exchanges,

irrespective of industry. Although the minimum requirement for Chanakya Fund AIF is 1 crore.

5. Regular Review and Rebalancing: Keep track of your portfolio's performance and make adjustments as needed. If one sector or size of company is performing exceptionally well, you might need to rebalance by selling some shares and investing in other sectors or asset classes to maintain diversification.

Diversifying with SME Stocks

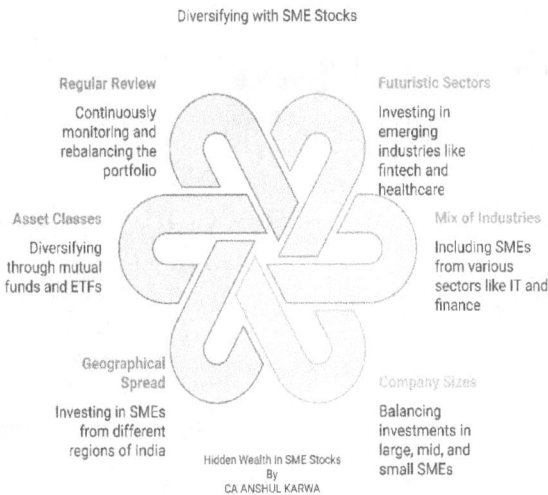

Regular Review
Continuously monitoring and rebalancing the portfolio

Futuristic Sectors
Investing in emerging industries like fintech and healthcare

Asset Classes
Diversifying through mutual funds and ETFs

Mix of Industries
Including SMEs from various sectors like IT and finance

Geographical Spread
Investing in SMEs from different regions of India

Company Sizes
Balancing investments in large, mid, and small SMEs

Hidden Wealth in SME Stocks
By
CA ANSHUL KARWA

Understanding Risk and Return:

Imagine you're deciding whether to invest in a small bakery or a big supermarket chain. The bakery might offer higher returns if it becomes popular, but it also carries more risk because it's smaller and might struggle to compete with larger businesses. On the other hand, the supermarket chain might be more stable but offer lower returns.

Diversification for Safety:

Now, think about a basket of fruits. If you put all your money in one type of fruit and it goes bad, you'll lose everything. But if you spread your money across different fruits, even if one goes bad, you'll still have others to rely on. Similarly, spreading your investments across different SMEs and other assets helps lower the risk.

For example, suppose you invested in a variety of SMEs like a technology startup, a healthcare company, and a manufacturing business. If the technology sector faces challenges, your investment in healthcare or manufacturing might balance out the losses.

Investment Horizon and Patience:

Let's say you plant a sapling. It takes time to grow into a tree and bear fruit. Similarly, SME investments might take time to grow and give you returns. Having a longer investment horizon, like waiting for the tree to grow, can help you ride out any bumps along the way and potentially enjoy higher returns.

Doing Your Homework:

Before Kirti decides to invest her money in any business, she needs to do some research. For example, let's say she's thinking about putting money into a local software company. Kirti should check if the company has good employees who know what they're doing, if they're making new, unique and interesting products, and if people like what they're selling. If everything looks good after checking these things, then it might be a smart move for Kirti to invest her money in that company.

Monitoring and Adjusting:

Just like driving a car, you need to keep an eye on your investments and make adjustments as needed. If you notice that one of your SME stocks is underperforming or facing challenges, you might need to reassess your investment and consider making changes to protect your money.

By following the above points, spreading your investments, being patient, doing thorough study and research, and staying careful, you can balance the risks and get rewards of investing in SMEs or even any other shares more effectively.

How to balance risk and return in SME investments?

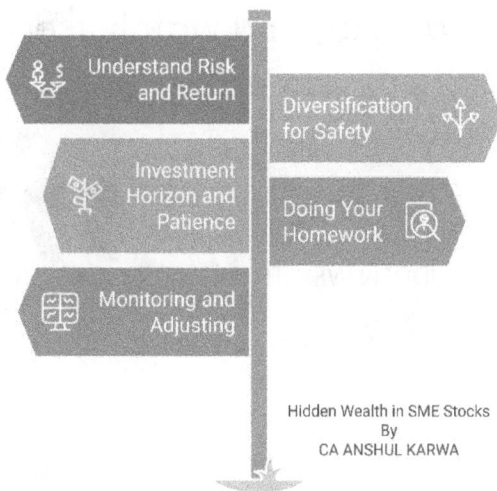

Understand Risk and Return

Diversification for Safety

Investment Horizon and Patience

Doing Your Homework

Monitoring and Adjusting

Hidden Wealth in SME Stocks
By
CA ANSHUL KARWA

"

Invest like a bull, sit like a bear, and watch like an eagle.

VIjay Kedia

HIDDEN WEALTH IN SME STOCKS
BY
CA ANSHUL KARWA

"

Chapter 7: Case studies of well-structured SME stock portfolios

Let's take two case studies of well-structured SME IPO stock portfolios in India:

Case Study 1: Technology Focus

Mr. Vinay Daga is an investor who believes in the potential of technology-driven SMEs in India. He carefully selects SME IPO stocks from the technology sector to build his portfolio.

1. Company A:

  - IPO: Quick Touch Technology Ltd.

  - Sector: Information Technology (IT)

  - Investment Thesis: Mr. Vinay invests in Quick Touch Technology Ltd. because of its innovative software solutions and strong management team. The company specializes in AI-driven products, which Mr. Vinay believes have significant growth potential in the digital era.

2. Company B:

   - IPO: Techknowgreen Solutions Ltd.

   - Sector: Information Technology (IT) &Software Services

   - Investment Thesis: Vinay sees potential in Techknowgreen Solutions Ltd. due to its focus on providing customized software services to businesses. The company has a solid client base and a reputation for delivering high-quality solutions, making it an attractive investment opportunity.

3. Company C:

 - IPO: Newjaisa Technologies Ltd.

 - Sector: Information Technology (IT) & Software Services

 - Investment Thesis: Vinay recognizes the promising prospects of Newjaisa Technologies Ltd. because of its specialization in tailoring software services for various businesses. With a strong clientele and a track record of delivering top-notch solutions, the company emerges as an appealing investment option.

Vinay carefully monitors each company's performance and adjusts his portfolio as needed. Over time, his well-structured SME IPO stock portfolio in the technology sector generates attractive returns, outperforming the market average.

Case Study 2: Diversified Approach

Mrs. Kunika is an investor who adopts a diversified approach by investing in SME IPO stocks across multiple sectors in India.

1. Company X:

  - IPO: Jainam Ferro Alloys Ltd.

  - Sector: Ferro Manganese alloys

  - Investment Thesis: Kunika is impressed by the potential of Jainam Ferro Alloys Ltd. in the Ferro Manganese industry. The company's focus on producing Ferro Manganese alloys tailored to specific industrial needs has caught his attention. With a solid customer base and a reputation for consistently delivering high-quality alloys, Jainam Ferro Alloys Ltd. stands out as an attractive investment opportunity in the market.

2. Company Y:

  - IPO: KN Agri Ltd.

  - Sector: Vegetable Oils & Products

  - Investment Thesis: Kunika is excited about the potential of KN Agri Resources Ltd. in the vegetable oils and products sector. The company's focus on making and selling vegetable oils and related products makes it a promising investment. With a strong market presence and a good reputation for quality, KN Agri Resources Ltd. looks like a great opportunity for investors.

3. Company C:

  - IPO: Cool Caps Industries Ltd.

  - Sector: Bottle Caps Manufacturing

- Investment Thesis: Kunika diversifies her portfolio by including Cool Caps Ltd., a company specializing in bottle caps manufacturing. She believes that the increasing demand for caps presents an opportunity for growth in this sector.

By adopting a diversified approach, Kunika reduces risk and maximizes potential returns from her SME IPO stock portfolio. Despite fluctuations in individual sectors, her portfolio maintains stability and delivers attractive short term to long term growth.

> **I started investing at the age of 11. I was late!**
>
> Warren Buffett

HIDDEN WEALTH IN SME STOCKS
BY
CA ANSHUL KARWA

Chapter 8: Government Initiatives and Regulations

Overview of government schemes supporting SMEs and their impact on stocks

This chapter might seem boring, and some of you might even want to skip it. But trust me, it's really important to understand what the government thinks about SMEs. Their policies and support can make a big difference, so don't miss this.

Government Initiatives and Regulations

Small and Medium Enterprises (SMEs) form the backbone of many economies, contributing significantly to economic growth, employment generation, and innovation. Recognizing their importance, governments worldwide implement various schemes and regulations to support SME development. In India, these initiatives play a crucial role in fostering the growth and sustainability of SMEs across diverse sectors.

Key Government Schemes Supporting SMEs:

1. MSME Development Act:

The Micro, Small, and Medium Enterprises Development (MSMED) Act, 2006, is a landmark legislation aimed at promoting the growth and competitiveness of SMEs in India. Under this act, MSMEs benefit from preferential treatment in terms of credit availability, technology upgradation, marketing support, and easier access to government procurement opportunities.

Example: The implementation of the MSMED Act has facilitated the growth of numerous SMEs across sectors such as manufacturing, services, and agriculture. For instance, small-scale manufacturing units involved in sectors like textiles, handicrafts, and agro-processing have received support in the form of credit facilities, technology interventions, and market linkages, leading to enhanced productivity and competitiveness.

Government Support for SMEs

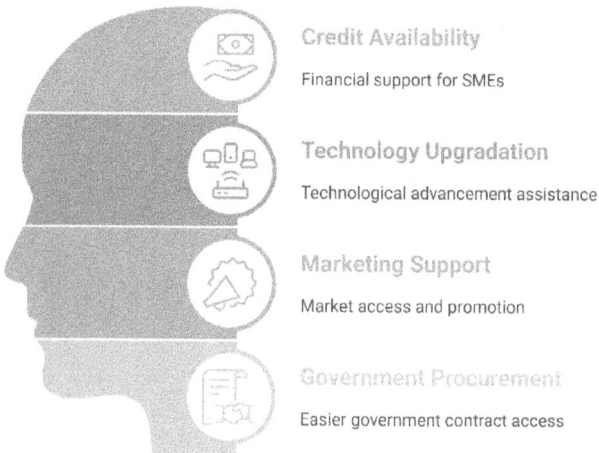

Credit Availability
Financial support for SMEs

Technology Upgradation
Technological advancement assistance

Marketing Support
Market access and promotion

Government Procurement
Easier government contract access

Hidden Wealth in SME Stocks
By
CA ANSHUL KARWA

2. Credit Guarantee Fund Scheme (CGTMSE):

The CGTMSE scheme aims to provide collateral-free credit facilities to micro and small enterprises by guaranteeing a portion of the loans extended by financial institutions. This initiative encourages banks and other lending institutions to extend credit to SMEs without the need for traditional collateral, thereby addressing one of the major challenges faced by small businesses—access to finance.

Example: Through the CGTMSE scheme, thousands of small businesses across India have been able to avail of bank loans without providing collateral security. For instance, a small textile manufacturing unit in Tamil Nadu might obtain a loan to invest in machinery and expand its production capacity, leveraging the

CGTMSE scheme's guarantee cover to mitigate the lender's risk.

3. Startup India Initiative:

Launched in 2016, the Startup India initiative aims to promote entrepreneurship and innovation by providing a conducive ecosystem for startups to thrive. This initiative offers various incentives, such as tax exemptions, funding support, simplification of regulatory procedures, and incubation facilities, to nurture the growth of startups across different sectors.

Example: Startups in the technology sector, such as software development firms, artificial intelligence startups, and e-commerce ventures, have benefited significantly from the Startup India initiative. For instance, a tech startup in

Bengaluru might receive funding support from government-backed venture capital funds and access mentorship programs to scale its operations and penetrate new markets.

4. Make in India Campaign:

The Make in India campaign aims to promote domestic manufacturing and position India as a global manufacturing hub. This initiative offers incentives, such as tax breaks, subsidies, infrastructure support, and ease of doing business reforms, to attract investments and foster the growth of manufacturing SMEs.

Example: Manufacturing SMEs operating in sectors like automotive components, electronics, and pharmaceuticals have leveraged the Make in India campaign to expand their production capacities, enhance product quality, and explore export opportunities. For instance, a small-scale automotive component manufacturer in Maharashtra might benefit from infrastructure support and export promotion schemes under the Make in India campaign to diversify its customer base and increase revenue.

5. Export Promotion Schemes:

Various export promotion schemes, such as the Export Promotion Capital Goods (EPCG) scheme, Merchandise Exports from India Scheme (MEIS), and Export Credit Guarantee Corporation (ECGC) schemes, aim to support SMEs in expanding their export markets and enhancing competitiveness globally. These schemes provide financial incentives, export credit insurance, and assistance in market access to promote SME exports.

Example: SMEs engaged in sectors like textiles, engineering goods, and pharmaceuticals have capitalized on export promotion schemes to access international markets and boost exports. For instance, a small textile exporter in Gujarat might benefit from financial incentives and export credit insurance under the MEIS and ECGC schemes to mitigate export-related risks and expand its business globally.

Government Support for SME's

MSME Development Act

CGTMSE Scheme

Startup India Initiative

Make in India Campaign

Export Promotion Schemes

Hidden Wealth in SME Stocks
By
CA ANSHUL KARWA

Impact of Government Initiatives on Stocks:

1. Boost in Investor Confidence:

Government schemes supporting SMEs often boost investor confidence in the sector, leading to increased investment inflows into SME stocks. Positive announcements regarding policy reforms, incentives, and support measures can drive up stock prices of SMEs, reflecting investor optimism about the sector's growth prospects.

Example: Following the announcement of the Startup India initiative, shares of listed startups and technology-driven SMEs witnessed a surge in investor interest, leading to a rally in stock prices. Investors viewed the government's support for startups as a positive development, fueling expectations of robust growth and profitability in the sector.

2. Improved Access to Funding:

Government initiatives such as the CGTMSE scheme facilitate easier access to funding for SMEs, enabling them to expand their operations, invest in technology upgradation, and fuel growth. This improved access to finance positively impacts the financial performance and stock prices of SMEs, as investors perceive enhanced liquidity and growth potential.

Example: SMEs availing loans under the CGTMSE scheme may utilize the funds to finance expansion projects, upgrade production facilities, or diversify product offerings. As these investments translate into higher revenues and profitability, SME stocks may witness upward price movements, reflecting investor confidence in the companies' growth prospects.

3. Enhanced Competitiveness:

Government initiatives focused on skill development, technology upgradation, and infrastructure development contribute to the enhanced competitiveness of SMEs in domestic and international markets. SMEs that benefit from these initiatives may witness improvements in operational efficiency, market share, and profitability, leading to higher stock valuations.

Example: SMEs operating in sectors prioritized under government initiatives, such as manufacturing, exports, and technology, may gain a competitive edge through access to subsidized credit, export promotion schemes, and technological interventions. As these SMEs strengthen their market position and expand their customer base, their stocks may experience upward price trends, reflecting investor confidence in the companies' growth trajectory.

4. Regulatory Compliance and Governance:

Government regulations and compliance requirements play a crucial role in shaping the business environment for SMEs. Initiatives aimed at simplifying regulatory procedures, enhancing corporate governance standards, and promoting transparency contribute to increased investor trust and confidence in SME stocks.

Example: SMEs adhering to regulatory compliance requirements and adopting best practices in corporate governance may attract greater investor interest and command premium valuations in the stock market. Investors perceive companies with robust compliance frameworks as less susceptible to regulatory risks and governance-related issues, leading to higher stock prices and shareholder returns.

In conclusion, government initiatives and regulations have a significant impact on the performance and valuation of SME stocks. By understanding and leveraging these initiatives, investors can make informed investment decisions and capitalize on the growth potential of the SME sector in India. Additionally, policymakers play a crucial role in designing and implementing supportive policies that foster the sustainable development of SMEs, thereby contributing to economic growth, job creation, and wealth generation.

Regulatory considerations for investors in SME stocks

Regulatory considerations for investors in SME stocks are important because they help investors understand the rules and regulations that govern the trading and ownership of these stocks. Here are some key regulatory aspects to consider, explained in easy language with examples:

1. Listing Requirements: Before a company can offer its stocks to the public, it must meet certain listing requirements set by the regulatory authorities. These requirements ensure that the company is financially stable and transparent enough for public investment.

Example: The Securities and Exchange Board of India (SEBI) sets listing requirements for SMEs on stock exchanges like the BSE SME and NSE Emerge platforms. These requirements may include criteria related to minimum net worth, profitability, and corporate governance standards.

2. Disclosure Requirements: Listed companies, including SMEs, are required to disclose certain information to investors on a regular basis. This information helps investors make informed decisions about buying or selling stocks.

Example: SMEs are required to disclose financial statements, quarterly results, material developments, and other relevant information to the stock exchanges and regulatory authorities. This ensures transparency and accountability, allowing investors to assess the company's performance and prospects accurately.

3. Compliance with Regulations: SMEs must comply with various regulatory requirements, including corporate governance norms, insider trading regulations, and tax laws. Compliance with these regulations is essential for maintaining investor trust and avoiding legal issues.

Example: Companies must adhere to SEBI's regulations on corporate governance, which include appointing independent directors, establishing audit committees, and maintaining proper accounting practices. Non-compliance with these regulations can lead to penalties and loss of investor confidence.

4. Market Manipulation Prevention: Regulatory authorities enforce rules to prevent market manipulation and insider trading, which can distort stock prices and harm investors. These rules aim to maintain a fair and orderly market environment for all participants.

Example: SEBI prohibits insider trading, where company insiders use non-public information to trade stocks for their benefit. Similarly, SEBI monitors market activities to detect and prevent manipulation techniques like price rigging and stock cornering.

5. Investor Protection Measures: Regulatory authorities implement investor protection measures to safeguard the interests of investors in SME stocks. These measures include mechanisms for dispute resolution, grievance redressal, and investor education.

Example: SEBI operates an Investor Grievance Redressal Mechanism to address investor complaints related to SME stocks. Investors can file complaints through SEBI's SCORES platform, and SEBI ensures prompt resolution of grievances in a fair and transparent manner.

By understanding the regulatory framework helps investors assess the risks and opportunities associated with SME investments and navigate the stock market more effectively.

> **"**All intelligent investing
> is value investing —
> acquiring more than
> you are paying for.
>
> Charlie Munger **"**

HIDDEN WEALTH IN SME STOCKS
BY
CA ANSHUL KARWA

Chapter 9: Tips for Successful SME Stock Investing

Practical tips and advice for individuals looking to invest in SME stocks

1. Do Your Homework: Before investing in any SME stock, it's important to do your research. Look into the company's business model, financial health, management team, and growth prospects. For example, if you're considering investing in a local restaurant chain, visit their outlets, try their food, and assess customer reviews to gauge the company's popularity and potential for growth. But this is just an example, most of the times there are businesses which we cant visit/try, then do well research through internet and via social media.

2. Diversify Your Portfolio: Don't put all your eggs in one basket. Spread your investments across multiple SME stocks from different sectors and industries. This

helps reduce the risk of losing all your money if one company or sector performs poorly. For instance, if you invest in a technology startup, consider diversifying with a healthcare services company and a manufacturing SME to balance out your portfolio's risk.

3. Invest for the Long Term: Successful investing in SME stocks requires patience. Instead of trying to make quick profits, focus on long-term growth and value creation. For example, if you believe in the growth potential of a small software company, be prepared to hold onto your investment for several years to allow the company to grow and realize its full potential.

4. Stay Informed: Keep yourself updated on market trends, economic developments, and industry news. This

helps you make informed decisions about when to buy, sell, or hold onto your SME stocks. For example, if you hear about a new government initiative to promote renewable energy, it might be a good time to consider investing in SMEs operating in the clean energy sector.

5. Manage Risk: Investing in SME stocks carries inherent risks, so it's important to manage your risk exposure. Set realistic expectations and be prepared for ups and downs in the market. Consider using risk management techniques like stop-loss orders or diversification to protect your investments. For example, if you notice that one of your SME stocks is underperforming, you might consider selling some shares to limit your losses and reinvesting in other opportunities.

6. Stay Disciplined: Stick to your investment strategy and avoid making impulsive decisions based on emotions or short-term market fluctuations. Remember that successful investing requires discipline and a long-term perspective. For example, if the market experiences a downturn, resist the urge to panic sell your SME stocks and instead stay focused on your long-term investment goals.

By following these practical tips and staying disciplined in your approach, you can increase your chances of success when investing in SME stocks. Remember to do your research, diversify your portfolio, invest for the long term, stay informed, manage risk, and stay disciplined to achieve your financial goals.

Avoid these common traps

1. Overlooking Research:

Neglecting thorough research is a common mistake that can lead to investment losses. For example, suppose you're considering investing in a small software startup. Without researching the company's financial statements, customer base, and competition, you might miss crucial information about its growth prospects and risks. As a result, you could end up investing in a company with unsustainable growth or facing stiff competition.

2. Ignoring Diversification:

Failing to diversify your investment portfolio is another pitfall to avoid. For instance, imagine you decide to invest all your savings in a single SME stock because you believe in its potential. However, if that particular industry faces challenges or the company encounters financial difficulties, your entire investment could be at risk. Diversifying across different sectors, such as technology, healthcare, and consumer goods, can help mitigate this risk by spreading your investments.

3. Short-term Thinking:

Succumbing to short-term thinking and reacting impulsively to market fluctuations can hinder long-term investment success. For example, if the stock price of an SME you invested in drops suddenly, you might panic and sell your shares to cut losses. However, if you had conducted thorough research and believed in the company's long-term prospects, you might have stayed invested and eventually seen the stock price rebound.

4. Neglecting Risk Management:

Ignoring risk management practices is a significant pitfall that investors should avoid. For instance, suppose you invest a large portion of your savings in a speculative SME stock without considering the potential downside risks. If the company fails to deliver on its promises or faces regulatory issues, you could suffer significant losses. Implementing risk management strategies such as setting stop-loss orders or diversifying your investments can help protect your capital and minimize losses.

Real life examples:

Example 1:

Spectrum Talent Management Ltd., with a IPO price of Rs 160 but since launch it has declined to Rs 102.

This serves as a reminder that not all SME stocks perform as expected, and investing in them carries inherent risks.

Check the chart on next page:

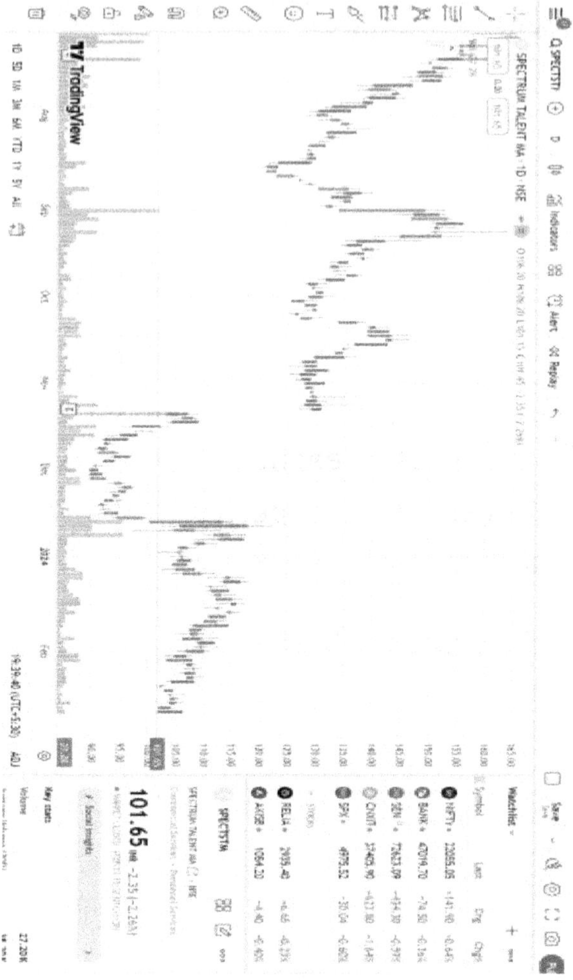
SPECTRUM TALENT MA · 1D · NSE
TradingView
Watchlist
101.65

Example 2:

Milestone Furniture Ltd., with a IPO price of Rs 45 but since launch it has declined to Rs 4.43. Check the chart below:

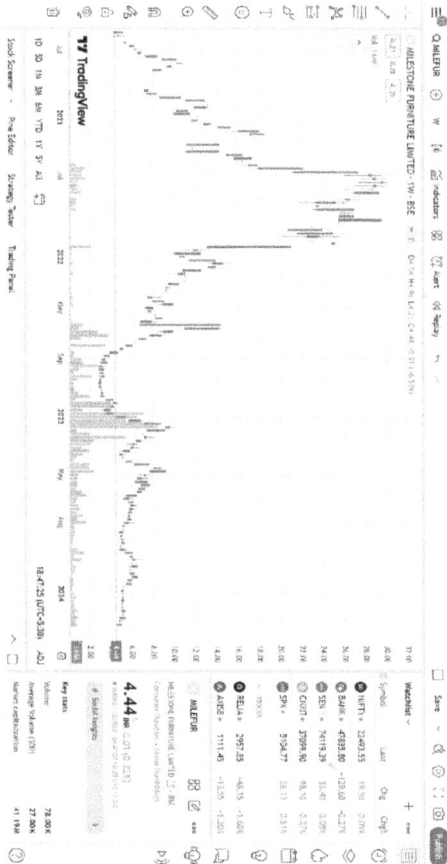

In conclusion, while SME stocks offer the potential for significant returns, investors should approach them with caution and diligence. Spectrum Talent Management Ltd. and Milestone Furniture Ltd. example serves as a valuable lesson that not all SME stocks will perform as expected, underscoring the importance of research and informed decision-making in the world of SME investing and the same is implied in large cap and mid cap stocks also.

> **Market fluctuations are your friend, not your enemy.**
>
> Warren Buffett

HIDDEN WEALTH IN SME STOCKS
BY
CA ANSHUL KARWA

Chapter 10: Learning from experienced investors in the SME segment

Let's check some real life Indian examples of investors in the SME segment, with some renowned names which you must have heard:

1. Rakesh Jhunjhunwala:

Everyone must have heard his name. He is known as the "Warren Buffett of India," Rakesh Jhunjhunwala is a renowned investor who has made significant investments in both large-cap and SME stocks. His success story serves as inspiration for many investors. Jhunjhunwala's investment philosophy emphasizes thorough research, patience, and conviction in his investment decisions.

Real Life Example: One notable investment by Jhunjhunwala was in Raghav Productivity Enhancers Ltd, a Jaipur based company specializing in manufacturing quartz based ramming mass. The company launched its IPO in 2016 at an issue price of ₹39 per share. Over the years, the stock has demonstrated significant growth, with its current market price exceeding ₹500.

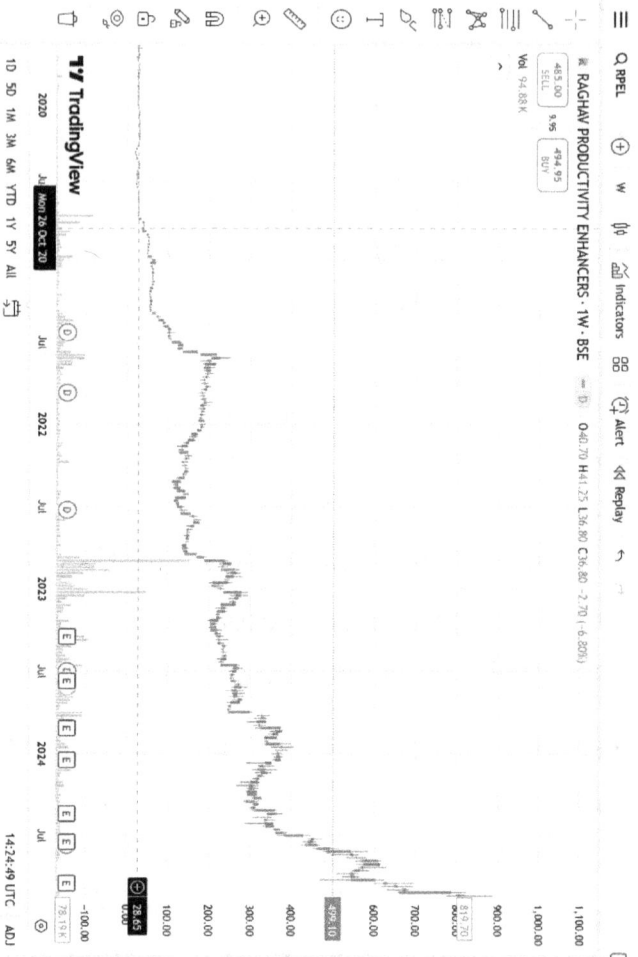

2. Vijay Kedia:

Vijay Kedia is another veteran investor known for his expertise in the Indian stock market. He has a keen eye for identifying multibagger stocks, including those in the SME segment. Kedia's investment approach focuses on identifying high-growth companies with strong fundamentals and management integrity.

Real life Example: Kedia's investment in Affordable Robotic & Automation Ltd. (ARAPL) highlights the potential of identifying promising companies early. ARAPL, specializing in automation solutions, launched its IPO in June 2018 at ₹85 per share. the stock has appreciated significantly, trading at above ₹500, reflecting a substantial return over the years.

Kedia's investment in Cera Sanitaryware Limited, a leading manufacturer of sanitaryware products, is noteworthy. While Cera started as an Small cap (not SME), it eventually grew into a well-established company with a strong market presence. Kedia's investment in Cera showcases the potential for long-term wealth creation by identifying and investing in promising SMEs.

Also, Kedia's investment in TAC Security, which went public with its IPO in April 2024. TAC Security, a company focused on cybersecurity, is in a growing industry as more and more businesses need strong protection against online threats. His decision shows how recognizing promising, up-and-coming businesses can lead to great opportunities for wealth creation over time. He made over 400% with it. IPO price of Rs 106 to latest price over Rs 1500.

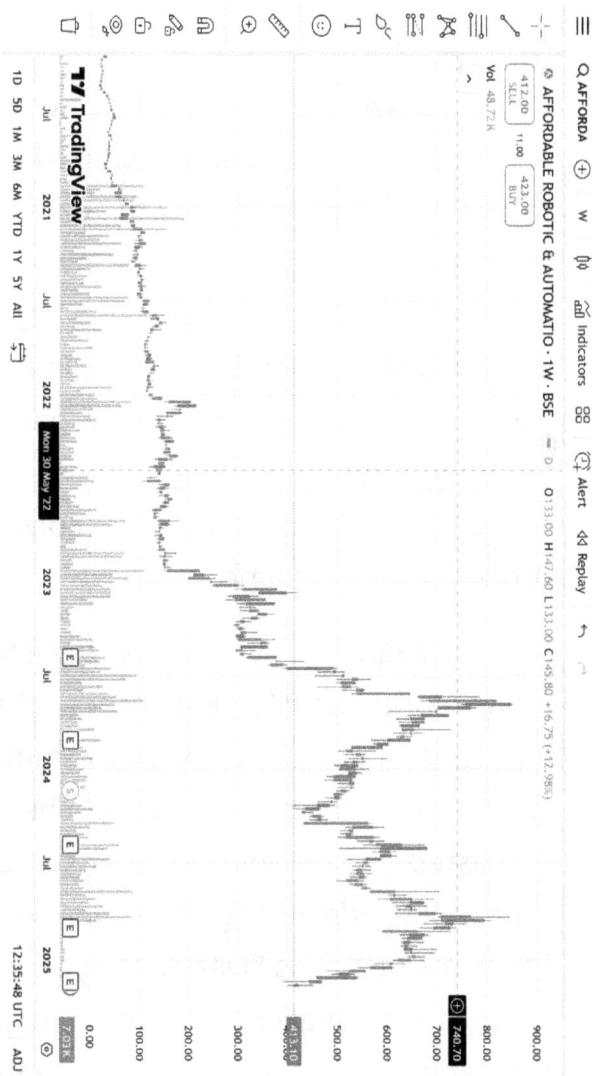

3. Mukul Agrawal:

Mukul Agrawal is a well-known investor in the Indian stock market, recognized for his ability to spot high-growth companies early. He follows a strategy of investing in businesses with strong fundamentals and high growth potential, including SME stocks. His approach focuses on patience, research, and staying invested in companies that show consistent performance over time.

Real life Example: Agrawal has invested in Raghav Productivity Enhancers Ltd., a company specializing in silica ramming mass used in the steel industry. The stock was listed at ₹39 and has now surged to over ₹500, delivering massive returns. Another example is Siyaram Recycling Ltd., a waste management and recycling company, where Agrawal saw potential in its sustainable business model and growth trajectory.

His investment strategy highlights the importance of identifying promising SMEs early and holding onto them for long-term wealth creation.

Now, their investment strategies, market insights, and success stories offer valuable guidance for navigating the complexities of the stock market and identifying promising investment opportunities in the SME segment.

Check the chart on next page.

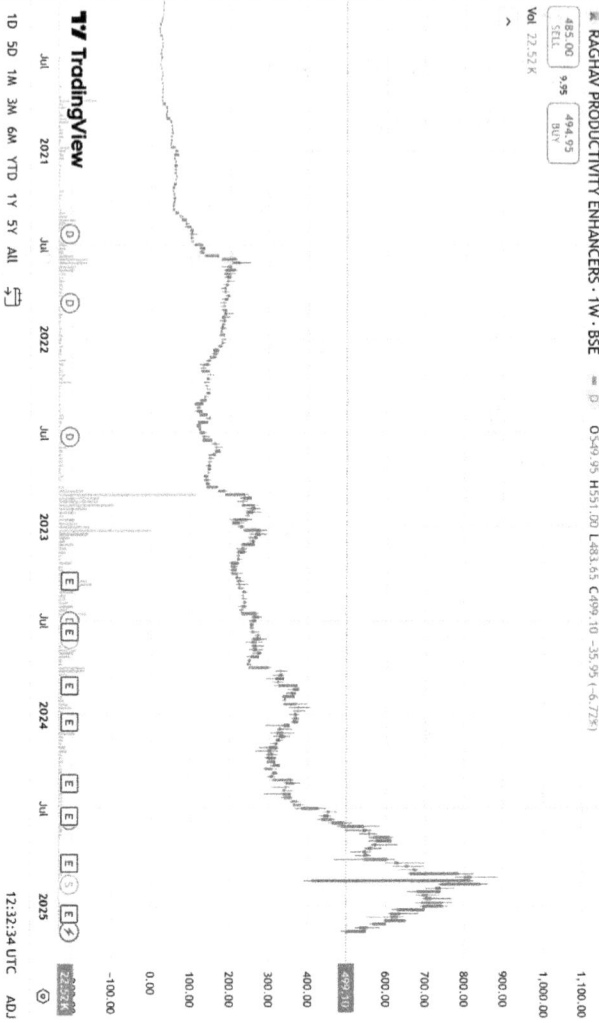

4. Anshul Karwa

I think till now you know I am an investor and with my over nine years of experience in the financial markets, I bring a unique blend of expertise to the world of stock market investments.

With a Chartered Accountant degree and a deep knowledge of market trends, when I stepped into the SME market, I was surprised to see how this hidden market was giving unbelievable returns. Let's take a look at my past year's stocks with a picture showing some shares from my SME portfolio.

1. Jainam Ferro Alloys Ltd:

I made a smart investment in Jainam Ferros, buying shares at around ₹70. In just six months, the stock price jumped to ₹202, and I decided to book my profits.

This means I earned a fantastic return of about 188.29%!

JAINAM-SM			Qty. 2000
Realised	+2,63,600.00 (+188.29%)		
Buy avg.	70.00	Buy value	1,40,000.00
Sell avg.	201.80	Sell value	4,03,600.00

2. Shera Energy Ltd:

I spotted a great opportunity in Shera Energy and bought shares at around ₹62.

In less than a year, the stock has climbed to ₹165, giving me a solid gain of about 164.35%! This shows my knack for picking strong SME stocks.

I'm still holding onto this gem, with a short-term target of ₹250+ and a long-term goal of ₹430-450-500.

Qty. 2000 • Avg. 62.55	+164.35%
SHERA-SM	+2,05,600.00
Invested 1,25,100.00	LTP 165.35 (-0.98%)

3. Systango Ltd:

I made a smart move by investing in Systango at ₹98.15. In less than a year, the stock has soared to ₹328, giving me an incredible gain of about 284.11%!

My patience and confidence in this stock have paid off well, and Systango still looks strong with great growth potential ahead.

SYSTANGO
Qty : 1600 @ Avg. 98.15

Invested : 1,57,040.00

LTP : 377.00 (+15.06%)
Today's P/L : 78,960.00
(15.06%)
Overall P/L : 4,46,160.00
(284.11%)

4. Lloyds Luxuries Ltd:

I invested in Lloyds Luxuries Ltd after analyzing its business potential. I bought 2 lots of shares and sold one, making an impressive 98.60% profit in just 3 months!

LLOYDS-SM   Qty 3000

Realised +1,27,200.00 (+98.60%)

Buy avg. 43.00   Buy value   1,29,000.00
Sell avg. 85.40   Sell value 2,56,200.00

I chose to keep the other lot in my long-term portfolio, confident in its future growth. It's still giving a solid gain of about 113.95%!

Investing is all about making smart decisions and grabbing the right opportunities at the right time.

LLOYDS

Qty : 3000 @ Avg. 42.99   LTP : 90.10 (-0.44%)
CMV : 2,70,300.00   Today's P/L : -1,200.00
                                           (-0.44%)
Invested : 1,28,970.00   Overall P/L : 1,41,330.00
                                           (109.58%)

5. Baheti Recycling Industries Ltd.:

Seeing a great opportunity in the Aluminium sector, I invested in Baheti Recycling Industries Ltd. at ₹45 per share during its IPO.

Watching the market closely, I noticed a strong uptrend and decided to make the most of it.

When the stock jumped to ₹120, I booked my profits, locking in a massive 166.67% gain, all within just a week!

BAHETI-SM   Qty. 3000

Realised +2,25,000.00 (+166.67%)

Buy avg.	45.00	Buy value	1,35,000.00
Sell avg.	120.00	Sell value	3,60,000.00

6. AGUL Ltd:

I saw a good opportunity in AGUL and bought shares at ₹60. As the stock gained momentum, I sold at ₹106.5, making a 77.5% profit within 2 months.

I used my skill in spotting and taking advantage of short-term market trends.

AGUL-ST   Qty. 2000

Realised +92,100.00 (+76.75%)

Buy avg. 60.00   Buy value   1,20,000.00
Sell avg. 106.05   Sell value 2,12,100.00

> **You make most of your money in a bear market; you just don't realize it at the time.**
>
> Shelby Cullom Davis

HIDDEN WEALTH IN SME STOCKS
BY
CA ANSHUL KARWA

Chapter 11: How I Select and Invest in SME Stocks

How I Select My Stocks

1. **Focus on Futuristic Sectors**: Invest in industries expected to grow, like electric vehicles (EVs), solar energy, and technology. For example, *Oriana Power* specializes in solar energy solutions, aligning with the global shift towards renewable energy.

2. **Check Growth Numbers**: Look for companies showing strong growth in sales and profits. *Lancer Container Lines*, a logistics company, has demonstrated consistent revenue growth, indicating a healthy business trajectory.

3. **Understand Leadership Plans**: Research the company's leaders to see if they have clear and ambitious plans. *Gensol Engineering*, operating in the renewable energy sector, has leadership committed to expanding its services, reflecting a strong vision for growth.

4. **Review Order Book**: A company's order book shows pending orders, indicating future revenue. *Omfurn India*, a furniture manufacturer, reported an order book of Rs. 95 crores, which suggests a steady upcoming business.

5. **Consider Company Size**: Investing in companies with a market capitalization between Rs. 50 to 2,000 crores can offer significant growth potential. *Waaree Renewable Technologies*, once an SME, grew substantially and moved to the mainboard, exemplifying this potential.

6. **Analyse Price to Earnings (P/E) Ratio or Forward P/E Ratio**: This ratio compares a company's share price to its earnings. A reasonable P/E ratio, combined with strong growth, can indicate a good investment. For example, *NACDAC Infrastructure* saw its stock price surge, reflecting positive market sentiment.

7. Special Situations: Look for SME companies with strong order books, recent fundraisings, notable investments from famous investor or individuals, plans for expansion, or involvement in mergers and acquisitions. These factors can signal potential growth and profitability.

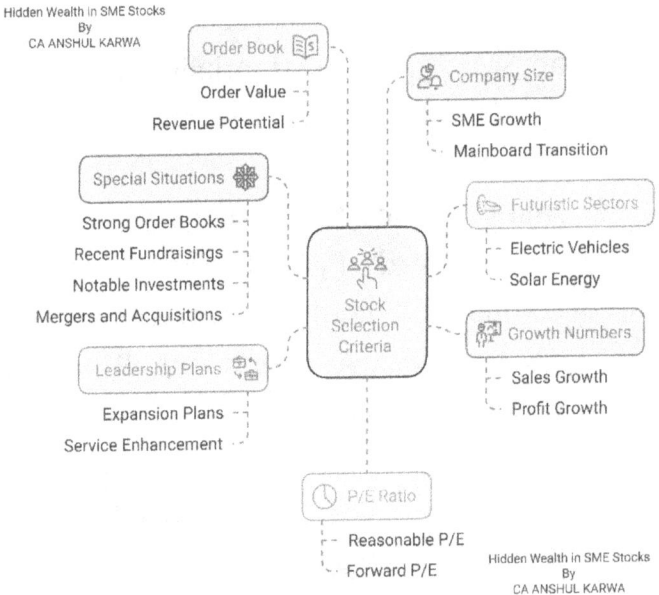

> **Market fluctuations are your friend, not your enemy.**
>
> Warren Buffett

HIDDEN WEALTH IN SME STOCKS
BY
CA ANSHUL KARWA

Chapter 12: My Top 10 Picks of SME Stocks

10 Picks of SME Stocks

1. Chaman Metallics Ltd: Based in Chandrapur, Maharashtra, Chaman Metallics Ltd specializes in the production of sponge iron. With six manufacturing plants across Chhattisgarh and Maharashtra, the company has rapidly emerged as a significant player in India's steel industry. Their commitment to operational excellence and strategic expansion underscores their growth trajectory.

2. Siyaram Recyclers Ltd: Specializing in waste management and recycling, Siyaram Recyclers Ltd is committed to environmental sustainability. The company focuses on converting waste into reusable materials, contributing to a cleaner environment.

3. Karnika Industries Ltd: Operating in the textiles sector, Karnika Industries Ltd is headquartered in Kolkata. The company focuses on the production of fabrics, catering to a diverse clientele. Since its IPO, Karnika Industries has demonstrated robust financial performance, reflecting its strong market position and commitment to quality.

4. Kore Digital Ltd: Operating in the digital infrastructure sector, Kore Digital Ltd provides comprehensive solutions for telecommunications and data services. Their expertise includes the development and maintenance of fiber-optic networks, supporting the growing demand for high-speed internet connectivity.

5. Kaushalya Logistics Ltd: Based in New Delhi, Kaushalya Logistics Ltd offers comprehensive logistics solutions, including transportation and supply chain management. The company's strategic location and efficient services have positioned it well within the logistics industry. Their focus on timely delivery and customer satisfaction has fostered a loyal client base

6. Shera Energy Ltd: Based in Jaipur Shera Energy Ltd is engaged in the manufacturing of winding wires and strips made from non-ferrous metals like copper and aluminum. Serving the electrical industry for over two decades, the company has built a reputable presence in the copper and aluminum winding wire and strips sector. Their dedication to quality and innovation has solidified their standing in the market.

7. Oriana Power Ltd: Oriana Power Ltd is a key player in the renewable energy sector, specializing in solar power solutions. The company offers end-to-end services, from designing and installing solar power systems to providing ongoing maintenance, promoting the adoption of clean energy.

8. KN Agri Ltd: KN Agri Ltd specializes in vegetable oils and related products, offering quality products to meet the evolving needs of consumers.

9. Bondada Engineering Ltd: Bondada Engineering Ltd offers a range of engineering and infrastructure services, including project management, construction, and maintenance. Their diverse portfolio spans multiple sectors, showcasing their versatility and commitment to quality.

10. Insolation Energy Limited: The company was established in 2015 in Jaipur, Rajasthan, is a prominent Indian company specializing in the production of solar energy solutions under the brand name INA. The company's product range includes solar photovoltaic (PV) modules, solar power conditioning units (PCUs), and solar batteries.

10 Picks of
SME Stocks

Chaman Metallics Ltd — Specializes in sponge iron production in Maharashtra.

Focuses on waste management and recycling for sustainability. — Siyaram Recyclers Ltd

Karnika Industries Ltd — Produces fabrics and serves a diverse clientele in textiles.

Provides telecommunications and data services solutions. — Kore Digital Ltd

Kaushalya Logistics Ltd — Offers logistics solutions including transportation and supply chain.

Manufactures winding wires and strips for the electrical industry. — Shera Energy Ltd

Oriana Power Ltd — Specializes in solar power solutions and maintenance services.

Offers quality vegetable oils and related products. — KN Agri Ltd

Bondada Engineering Ltd — Provides engineering and infrastructure services across sectors.

Insolation Energy Limited

Hidden Wealth in SME Stocks by CA ANSHUL KARWA

Disclaimer:

Please note that the stock suggestions provided are merely recommendations based on my analysis and understanding. It's very important to conduct your own research and seek professional advice before making any investment decisions. These suggestions are not to be taken as financial advice or tips and is solely for study purpose.

> Rule No. 1: Never lose money. Rule No. 2: Never forget rule No. 1.

Warren Buffett

HIDDEN WEALTH IN SME STOCKS
BY
CA ANSHUL KARWA

Conclusion

Since we are at the end of this book, let's see what we have covered. In this book, we've explored the exciting world of Indian Small and Medium Enterprises (SMEs) and uncovered the potential for wealth creation that lies within these often-overlooked gems of the Indian market.

Throughout the pages, you've learned about the unique opportunities and challenges associated with investing in SME stocks. From understanding the importance of thorough research and due diligence to discovering the top 10 picks of SME stocks, you've gained valuable insights to help you navigate this dynamic and rewarding sector.

Remember, investing in SME stocks requires patience, discipline, and a long-term perspective. While the journey may have its ups and downs, the potential for unseen riches and financial success is within reach for those who are willing to put in the effort and make informed decisions.

As you start on your own SME investment journey, always remember to stay informed, diversify your portfolio, and seek the advice of qualified professionals when needed. With dedication and perseverance, you have the opportunity to unlock hidden wealth and achieve your financial goals through SME stocks.

Thank you for joining me on this exploration of hidden wealth, and may your future endeavours in SME investing be filled with prosperity and success!

Also, I invite you to share it with your family, friends and colleagues who may also benefit from the knowledge and strategies outlined in this book. By spreading the word about the potential for wealth creation in SME stocks, you not only help others discover hidden opportunities but also contribute to building a community of informed investors.

Thank you for your support, and may your journey to financial success be shared and celebrated with those around you!

I value your input and welcome any suggestions or feedback you may have regarding this book or any other questions. Your insights are invaluable in helping me improve future editions and better serve the needs of readers like you. Please feel free to reach out to me at **caanshul@mail.ca.in** with your comments, questions, or ideas. I look forward to hearing from you!

Listing Process:

If you're interested in exploring how to list SME IPOs or have questions about the process, or want to list your company on Indian stock market, feel free to reach out to me. I'm here to assist and provide guidance to individuals and companies interested in navigating the SME IPO listing process.

You can contact me at **caanshul@mail.ca.in** for further information or to discuss your specific needs. I look forward to the opportunity to assist you!

Links to my social media accounts:

- https://in.linkedin.com/in/anshulkarwa
- https://www.quora.com/profile/Anshul-Karwa
- https://www.instagram.com/anshulkarwa/
- https://twitter.com/ianshulk

Seize the opportunity to invest in a company on the rise, and ride the journey from startup to success.

- CA ANSHUL KARWA